Thoreau and the Art of Life

Thoreau and the Art of Life

Reflections on Nature and the Mystery of Existence

Edited and with an introduction by
Roderick MacIver

Published by   and   Heron Dance Press and Art Studio
North Atlantic Books   179 Rotax Road
Berkeley, California   North Ferrisburgh, Vermont 05473
                                              888-304-3766
                                              www.herondance.org

Cover design by Brad Greene
Cover art "Traversing the Hills" and watercolors throughout
   by Roderick MacIver of Heron Dance
Printed in the United States of America

Thoreau and the Art of Life: Reflections on Nature and the Mystery of Existence is sponsored and published by the Society for the Study of Native Arts and Sciences (dba North Atlantic Books), an educational nonprofit based in Berkeley, California, that collaborates with partners to develop cross-cultural perspectives, nurture holistic views of art, science, the humanities, and healing, and seed personal and global transformation by publishing work on the relationship of body, spirit, and nature.

North Atlantic Books' publications are available through most bookstores. For further information, visit our website at www.northatlanticbooks.com or call 800-733-3000.

Library of Congress Cataloging-in-Publication Data

Thoreau, Henry David, 1817–1862.
    [Selections. 2009]
    Thoreau and the art of life : reflections on nature and the mystery of existence / edited and with an introduction by Roderick MacIver.
        p. cm.
    Includes bibliographical references.
    ISBN 978-1-55643-883-7
    1. Thoreau, Henry David, 1817-1862—Quotations. 2. Conduct of life. I. MacIver, Roderick. II. Title.
    PS3042.M18 2009
    818'.309—dc22
                                                                2009018879

5 6 7 8 9 VERSA 18 17 16 15

I dedicate this book to John Davis,
wild soul, backwoods wanderer,
protector of wild places and wildlife,
as good a friend as a man can have,
and an inspiration to me.

Acknowledgments

I would like to acknowledge the impact on this work of Walt McLaughlin of Wood Thrush Books, E.B. White and his wonderful essay *A Slight Sound at Evening*, Joseph Wood Krutch for his introduction to an edition of *Walden*, and Odell Shepard for his book *The Heart of Thoreau's Journals*. I also would like to express appreciation for the good work of the Thoreau Society and the Walden Woods Project.

Henry David Thoreau (1817–1862)

Chronology

1817	Thoreau is born in Concord, Massachusetts.
1835	Ralph Waldo Emerson (1803–1882) takes up residence in Concord.
1836	The Transcendental Club is founded.
1837	Thoreau graduates from Harvard, gives commencement speech.
1837	Thoreau teaches briefly in Concord but resigns to protest the disciplinary whipping of students. He reads Emerson's *Nature* twice in 1837—first in April, then again in June. Thoreau begins journal writing at Emerson's prompting.
1838	Thoreau works in his family's pencil factory and then opens a private school in Concord with his brother John.
1839	Thoreau takes a trip with his brother John down the Concord and Merrimack Rivers.
1840–44	*The Dial,* a transcendental journal edited by Margaret Fuller (1810–1850) and Emerson, is published.
1841–43	Thoreau lives intermittently with the Emerson household, then for the rest of his life in his family home. He serves as a handyman and assistant to Emerson, helping to edit and contributing poetry and prose to *The Dial.*
1842	Thoreau's brother John dies of lockjaw.
1842	"Natural History of Massachusetts" is published.
1842	Nathaniel Hawthorne (1804–1864) meets Thoreau while living in Concord for three years.
1842	William Ellery Channing (1818–1901), a transcendentalist poet, marries Margaret Fuller's sister, Ellen. Ellery Channing was Thoreau's first biographer, publishing *Thoreau, the Poet-Naturalist* in 1873.
1845–47	Thoreau lives at Walden Pond from July 4, 1845, to September 6, 1847, on Emerson's land, near Concord.
1846	Thoreau spends a night in jail for refusing to pay six years of delinquent poll taxes, purportedly in opposition to the Mexican-American War.
1849	*A Week on the Concord and Merrimack Rivers,* the account of the trip he had taken with his brother John in 1839, is published.
1849	"Resistance to Civil Government" is published (later known as "On the Duty of Civil Disobedience" or simply "Civil Disobedience").
1850	Thoreau becomes a land surveyor.
1854	*Walden* is published.
1857	Thoreau meets John Brown and writes passionately in his defense.
1862	Thoreau dies of tuberculosis. He is buried in Sleepy Hollow Cemetery in Concord.

The images on the preceding pages are based on photographs taken early in Thoreau's adult life and a few months before his death.

It is chiefly through books that we enjoy intercourse with superior minds. In the best books, great men talk to us, give us their most precious thoughts, and pour their souls into ours.

—William Ellery Channing

Table of Contents

Mr. Thorow [sic] dined with us yesterday. He is a singular character—a young man with much wild original nature still remaining in him; and so far as he is sophisticated, it is in a way and method of his own. He is as ugly as sin, long-nosed, queer-mouthed, and with uncouth and somewhat rustic, although courteous manners, corresponding very well with such an exterior. But his ugliness is of an honest and agreeable fashion, and becomes him much better than beauty. He was educated, I believe, at Cambridge, and formerly kept school in this town; but for two or three years back, he has repudiated all regular modes of getting a living, and seems inclined to lead a sort of Indian life among civilized men—an Indian life, I mean, as respects the absence of any systematic effort for a livelihood. He has been for some time an inmate of Mr. Emerson's family; and, in requital, he labors in the garden and performs such other offices as may suit him—being entertained by Mr. Emerson for the sake of what true manhood there is in him. Mr. Thorow is a keen and delicate observer of nature—a genuine observer, which, I suspect, is almost as rare a character as even an original poet; and Nature, in return for his love, seems to adopt him as her especial child, and shows him secrets which few others are allowed to witness. He is familiar with beast, fish, fowl, and reptile, and has strange stories to tell of adventures, and friendly passages with these lower brethren of mortality. Herb and flower, likewise, wherever they grow, whether in garden, or wild wood, are his familiar friends. He is also on intimate terms with the clouds and can tell the portents of storms. It is a characteristic trait, that he has a great regard for the memory of the Indian tribes, whose wild life would have suited him so well; and strange to say, he seldom walks over a ploughed field without picking up an arrow-point, a spearhead, or other relic of the red men—as if their spirits willed him to be the inheritor of their simple wealth.

With all this he has more than a tincture of literature—a deep and true taste for poetry, especially the elder poets, although more exclusive than is desirable, like all other transcendentalists, so far as I am acquainted with them. He is a good writer—at least, he has written one good article, a rambling disquisition on Natural History in the last Dial,—which, he says, was chiefly made up from journals of his own observations.

—Nathaniel Hawthorne, writing in 1842, recording his first impressions of Thoreau
   when Thoreau was 24, from *The American Notebooks*

Introduction

His journals should not be permitted to be read by any, as I think they were not meant to be read. I alone might read them intelligently. To most others they would only give false impressions. I have never been able to understand what he meant by his life. Why did he care so much about being a writer? Why did he pay so much attention to his own thoughts? Why was he so dissatisfied with everyone else, etc.? Why was he so much interested in the river and the woods and the sky, etc.?... Something peculiar, I judge.

—William Ellery Channing, Thoreau's friend, writing after his death

Thoreau thought through our potential as human beings to live complete lives—lives that encompass joy, adventure, reflection, natural beauty, meaningful work, and relaxation. He thought and wrote about nature, about love and friendship, art and creativity, spirituality, aging and death, simplicity, wisdom. He tried to live his conclusions. He was deeply devoted to the craft of writing. From these roots emerged a powerful and contradictory body of work that continues to inspire and confuse us.

Thoreau's work is important in large part because our culture desperately needs the perspective of people who know and love nature. Ellery Channing wrote after Thoreau's death, "His habit was to go abroad a portion of each day, to the field or woods or the Concord River. . . . During many years he used the afternoon for walking, and usually set forth about half past two, returning at half past five." He carried a notebook and a small magnifying glass in order, he said, "to see what I have caught in my traps which I set for facts." There is the walking in the beauty, the rain, the cold, of course, but there is also the time for reflection, and that reflection is one of the reasons that Thoreau's work has endured.

Despite the many eloquent passages in his work on leisure and the art of relaxation, Thoreau slaved over his writing. His seventeen journals totaled two million words and were the basis of his twenty published books. He wrote *Walden* eight times over a period of nine years, and he continued to revise the page proofs and then the bound copies of the finished book. The result reads like a personal letter to a close friend.

Most of the selections I've chosen for this book come from Thoreau's journals, in part because they are less well known than his books. More importantly, the journals provide fascinating insight into his thought processes, into his raw, unedited feelings on the things that meant the most to him. "Noth-

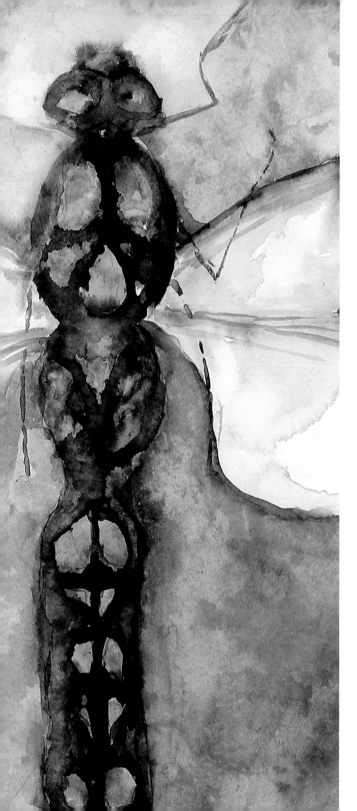

ing was ever so unfamiliar and startling to me as my own thoughts," he wrote. He also wrote, "My journal should be the record of my love. I would write in it only of the things I love, my affection for any aspect of the world, what I love to think of . . . I feel ripe for something . . . yet can't discover what that thing is. I feel fertile merely. It is seed time with me. I have lain fallow long enough."

Some biographers have pointed out that when he said he was living alone at Walden Pond he frequently went home to his mother for lunch. His antislavery position, his writing on civil disobedience, and his tendency toward misanthropy are also frequently discussed. I've heard his writing described as somewhat immature; I've even read that he was selfish, I assume because he lived alone and had little interest in a regular job. Thoreau also admitted to a tendency to exaggerate. He wrote to a friend, "I trust that you realize what an exaggerator I am—that I lay myself out to exaggerate whenever I have an opportunity." He exaggerated, he said, to emphasize. "You must speak loud to those who are hard of hearing." He went on to say, "Use me, by any means ye may find me serviceable."

I don't think *Walden* could have been written by someone who spent his entire life alone deep in the woods. *Walden* could have only come from someone with a varied life experience, someone who knew both

human society and solitude, nature and urban life, literature and wildflowers. In interviewing many dozens of people for the journal *Heron Dance* over the last several years, I've learned to pay particular attention to the contradictions. They provide a guide to the crucial issues at the center of a human life. Thoreau's contradictions are meaningful and telling. He believed fiercely in himself, yet considered himself to be a failure. His words on love are as profound and deeply felt as was his disdain for the general direction of human culture. He said that he wasn't interested in doing good or changing humanity: "As for doing good, I have tried it fairly, and strange as it may seem, am satisfied that it does not agree with my constitution." And, he said, "I came into this world not chiefly to make this a good place to

be in, but to live in it, be it good or bad." But through his words, carefully written and rewritten, making the world a better place—helping humanity see the error of its ways—is exactly what he was trying to do. Thoreau walked in the beauty and peace of the woods near Concord, Massachusetts, and thought about the rapidly changing society around him as industrialization gained momentum. He told us that business was people buying and selling and wasting their lives as serfs. And yet he was involved in the family business and invented or developed significant improvements in pencil graphite, grinding machines used in pencil manufacture, pipe-forming machines, and water wheels. These innovations transformed the American pencil industry and contributed in a major way to the success of the family business. When signing his name to something, Thoreau usually added the words "Civil Engineer."

What inspires me is that he dreamed his dream and he had the courage and discipline to live it. When his dream needed amendment, he amended it. Thoreau's writing challenges the decisions I make yearly, monthly, daily about the balance between work

and spending time in the woods. His thoughts on the quiet desperation of industrial humanity, on the crude bargain at the center of life in industrial society, and on what gives life value have led me to examine my life. More than once I've cringed at his words: "It is a characteristic of wisdom not to do desperate things." However difficult I find it to paint a picture that represents my love of wild places, I find it more difficult to live a life that is artful in its design and execution. I am particularly challenged by these words:

> It is something to be able to paint a particular picture, or to carve a statue, and so to make a few objects beautiful, but it is more glorious to carve and paint the very atmosphere and medium through which we look, which morally we can do. To affect the quality of the day, that is the highest of arts. We are tasked to make our lives, even in their details, worthy of the contemplation of our most elevated and critical hour.

It is some consolation to know that Thoreau, too, struggled to make his life a work of art, and he didn't always succeed. The exaggerations, contrasts, and contradictions should not detract from an appreciation of his work. Any life lived fully and completely, with energy and openness, has contradictions. Thoreau's work makes a difference because it

challenges us. It asks us to live our own truths with joy
and discipline. It asks us to recognize that we live in a
world larger than just the human world—a world and
universe of great beauty, mystery, and wonder.

❖ ❖ ❖

Many of Thoreau's journal entries are undated—in
particular the entries from the 1840s, when he was
in his twenties and early thirties, which was his peak
in terms of creative output. (Thoreau went to live at
Walden Pond in 1845 at the age of 28; *Walden* was
published in 1854.) Rather than end every undated
entry with "Journal entry, date unknown," the undated
entries do not have a credit line.

Similarly, I ask the reader's understanding in those
instances in which the quote I've selected actually
came from one of Thoreau's books and is not cred-
ited. I've been reading Thoreau for over twenty years
and only recently decided to consolidate my favorite
selections into book form. So for twenty years I've
been jotting down excerpts and quotes, often without
noting their source. While working on the manuscript
of this book, I came across selections that I was sure
came from *Walden,* for instance, but have been unable
to find them again in the book or on the Internet.

Roderick MacIver

Precepts and Principles

The precepts and principles that follow resulted from my efforts to distill from Thoreau's huge body of work the underlying simplicity. I wanted something manageable to work with as I think through my own life.

❖ *Everything worthwhile in life requires love, faith, and imagination. Friendship, love, imagination, a spiritual life, a close connection to the natural world—all are mysterious and difficult to put into words.*

❖ *Art emerges out of our inner life.*

❖ *The processes of life coexist with the processes of death. Good health, and life itself, are temporary.*

❖ *Society is a contrived reality. Expediency is valued; truth is not.*

❖ *Elements of a quality life: live simply, do quality work that is not rushed, avoid waste, live below your means, and keep a reserve. Set aside a substantial portion of your time for leisure.*

❖ *A close relationship with nature contributes joy and peace to a human life. Simple living enhances our awareness of, and openness to, the beauty of the natural world.*

❖ *A spiritual life is a life of calmness, of openness to mystery, beauty, and infinity.*

❖ *Long, frequent walks in the woods bring peace and serenity to a human life.*

❖ *Wisdom and simplicity are closely related.*

❖ *The path of joy is one of knowing who you are and living it. It requires befriending yourself.*

❖ *Make time for silence. Adopt a thoughtful rhythm to your work and life.*

Love and Friendship

Everything worthwhile in life requires love, faith, and imagination. All three are mysterious and difficult to put into words.

Thoreau's writing, and in particular his journal entries, offer deeply profound thoughts on love and friendship. The subject obviously meant a lot to him. He was an extremely sensitive man, and that sensitivity is reflected in all his writing, including that which expresses doubts about the goodness of humanity and the long-term potential of our species.

A friend is one who incessantly pays us the compliment of expecting from us all the virtues, and who can appreciate them in us. The friend asks no return but that his friend will religiously accept and wear and not disgrace his apotheosis of him. They cherish each other's hopes. They are kind to each other's dreams.

It is usually the imagination that is wounded first, rather than the heart—it being much more sensitive.

I only desire sincere relations with the worthiest of my acquaintance, that they may give me an opportunity once in a year to speak the truth.

The most I can do for my friend is simply to be his friend. I have no wealth to bestow on him. If he knows that I am happy in loving him, he will want no other reward. Is not friendship divine in this?

Friendship is never established as an understood relation. It is a miracle which requires constant proofs. It is an exercise of the purest imagination and of the rarest faith.

Those whom we can love, we can hate; to others we are indifferent.

Love must be as much a light as a flame.

Love is an attempt to change a piece of a dreamworld into reality.

True friendship can afford true knowledge. It does not depend on darkness and ignorance.

You know about a person who deeply interests you more than you can be told. A look, a gesture, an act, which to everybody else is insignificant, tells you more about that one than words can.

I lose my respect for the man who can make the mystery of sex the subject of a coarse jest, yet when you speak earnestly and seriously on the subject, is silent.

The kindness I have longest remembered has been of this sort, the sort unsaid; so far behind the speaker's lips that almost it already lay in my heart. It did not have far to go to be communicated.

There is more of good nature than of good sense at the bottom of most marriages.

In the love of narrow souls I make many short voyages but in vain—I find no sea room—but in great souls I sail before the wind without a watch, and never reach the shore.

The language of friendship is not words but meanings.

Between whom there is hearty truth, there is love.

There is no remedy for love but to love more.
        —Journal entry, 1839

Friends do not live in harmony merely, as some say, but in melody.
        —Journal entry, 1841

The heart is forever inexperienced.
        —*A Week on the Concord and Merrimack Rivers*, 1849

How often we find ourselves turning our backs on our actual friends, that we may go and meet their ideal cousins.
        —*A Week on the Concord and Merrimack Rivers*, 1849

In human intercourse the tragedy begins, not when there is misunderstanding about words, but when silence is not understood.
        —*A Week on the Concord and Merrimack Rivers*, 1849

It is hard for a man to take money from his friends, or any service. This suggests how all men should be related.
        —Journal entry, 1852

Nature must be viewed humanly to be viewed at all; that is, her scenes must be associated with humane affections, such as are associated with one's native place, for instance. She is most significant to a lover. A lover of Nature is preeminently a lover of man. If I have no friend, what is Nature to me? She ceases to be morally significant.

—Journal entry, 1852

Could a greater miracle take place than for us to look through each other's eyes for an instant?

—*Walden*, "Economy," 1854

Love is a thirst that is never slaked. Under the coarsest rind, the sweetest meat. If you would read a friend aright, you must be able to read through something thicker and opaquer than horn. If you can read a friend, all languages will be easy to you. Enemies publish themselves. They declare war. The friend never declares his love.

—Journal entry, 1856

And now another friendship is ended. I do not know what has made my friend doubt me, but I know that in love there is no mistake, and that every estrangement is well-founded.

—Journal entry, February 8, 1857

A man cannot be said to succeed in this life who does not satisfy one friend.

—Journal entry, February 19, 1857

Art, Creativity, and Writing

Art emerges out of our inner life.

Our moments of inspiration are not lost though we have no particular poem to show for them; for those experiences have left an indelible impression, and we are ever and anon reminded of them.

Write while the heat is in you. The writer who postpones the recording of his thoughts uses an iron which has cooled to burn a hole with. He cannot inflame the minds of his audience.

Nothing goes by luck in composition. It allows of no tricks. The best you can write will be the best you are.

When I hear the hypercritical quarreling about grammar and style, the position of the particles, etc., etc., stretching or contracting every speaker to certain rules of theirs . . . I see that they forget that the first requisite and rule is that expression shall be vital and natural, as much as the voice of a brute or an interjection: first of all, mother tongue; and last of all, artificial or father tongue. Essentially your truest poetic sentence is as free and lawless as a lamb's bleat.

Books, not which afford us a cowering enjoyment, but in which each thought is of unusual daring; such as an idle man cannot read, and a timid one would not be entertained by, which even make us dangerous to existing institutions—such call I good books.

The pleasure we feel in music springs from the obedience which is in it.

The poet is a man who lives at last by watching his moods. An old poet comes at last to watch his moods as narrowly as a cat does a mouse.

When I hear music, I fear no danger. I am invulnerable. I see no foe. I am related to the earliest times, and to the latest.

Hard and steady and engrossing labor with the hands, especially out of doors, is invaluable to the literary man and serves him directly. Here I have been for six days surveying in the woods, and yet when I get home at evening, somewhat weary at last, and beginning to feel that I have nerves, I find myself more susceptible than usual to the finest influences, as music and poetry. The very air can intoxicate me, or the least sight or sound, as if my finer senses had acquired an appetite by their fast.

Shortly after James Russell Lowell became editor of The Atlantic Monthly, *he removed from Thoreau's essay "Chesuncook" a sentence about a pine tree, which he thought would offend some readers: "It is as immortal as I am, and perchance will go to as high a heaven, there to tower above me still."*

Thoreau responded with a letter demanding that the sentence be put back in and calling the edit mean and cowardly. You have "no more right to omit a sentiment than to insert one, or put words into my mouth. . . . I should not read many books if I thought that they had been thus expurgated. I feel this treatment to be an insult, though not intended as such, for it presumes that I can be hired to suppress my opinions."

The Artist is he who detects and applies the law from observation of the works of Genius, whether of man or Nature. The Artisan is he who merely applies the rules which others have detected.

—Journal entry, 1849

How vain it is to sit down to write when you have not stood up to live.

—Journal entry, 1851

For a year or two past, my *publisher,* falsely so called, has been writing from time to time to ask what disposition should be made of the copies of *A Week on the Concord and Merrimack Rivers* still on hand, and at last suggesting that he had use for the room they occupied in his cellar. So I had them all sent to me here, and they have arrived today by express, filling the man's wagon—706 copies out of an edition of 1,000 which I bought of Munroe four years ago and have ever since been paying for, and have not quite paid for yet. The wares are sent to me at last, and I have an opportunity to examine my purchase. They are something more substantial than fame, as my back knows, which has borne them up two flights of stairs to a place similar to that to which they trace their origin. Of the remaining two hundred and ninety and odd, seventy-five were given away, the rest sold. I have now a library of nearly nine hundred volumes, over seven hundred of which I wrote myself.

—Journal entry, October 27, 1853.
   Thoreau lost $275 on the book; he paid $290 for unsold copies and received royalties of only $15.

I should not talk so much about myself if there were anybody else whom I knew as well. Unfortunately, I am confined to this theme by the narrowness of my experience. Moreover, I, on my side, require of every writer, first or last, a simple and sincere account of his own life, and not merely what he has heard of other men's lives; some such account as he would send to his kindred from a distant land; for if he has lived sincerely, it must have been in a distant land to me.

—*Walden,* "Economy," 1854

Each thought that is welcomed and recorded is a nest egg, by the side of which more will be laid.

—Journal entry, 1854

My faults are:—

Paradoxes,—saying just the opposite,—a style which may be imitated.

Ingenious.

Playing with words,—getting the laugh,—not always simple, strong, and broad.

Using current phrases and maxims, when I should speak for myself.

Not always earnest.

"In short," "in fact," "alas!" etc.

Want of conciseness.

—Journal entry, fall 1855

It has come to this—that the lover of art is one, and the lover of nature another, though true art is but the expression of our love of nature. It is monstrous when one cares but little about trees but much about Corinthian columns, and yet this is exceedingly common.

—Journal entry, 1857

There is always some accident in the best things, whether thoughts or expressions or deeds. The memorable thought, the happy expression, the admirable deed are only partly ours. The thought came to us because we were in a fit mood; also we were unconscious and did not know that we had said or done a good thing. We must walk consciously only partway toward our goal, and then leap in the dark to our success.

—Journal entry, March 11, 1858

I have many affairs to attend to, and feel hurried these days. Great works of art have endless leisure for a background, as the universe has space. Time stands still while they are created. The artist cannot be in [a] hurry. The earth moves round the sun with inconceivable rapidity, and yet the surface of the lake is not ruffled by it.

—Journal entry, 1859

A man receives only what he is ready to receive, whether physically or intellectually or morally, as animals conceive at certain seasons their kind only. We hear and apprehend only what we already half know.

—Journal entry, 1860

Aging, Disease, Death

*The processes of life coexist with the processes of death. Good health,
and life itself, are temporary.*

*Death touched Thoreau's life in profound ways.
Tuberculosis claimed at least one member of most
families in Concord, including Henry's father and sister
and the first wife of his friend Ralph Waldo Emerson.
Ultimately, at the age of 44, Henry died of it too.*

*Thoreau's older brother John died in his arms
of lockjaw (tetanus), the result of a small cut during
shaving, when Henry was 25. Thoreau was an
extremely sensitive man, and shortly after his brother's
death, he developed symptoms of lockjaw in sympathy.*

I suppose you think that persons who are as old as
your father and myself are always thinking about very
grave things, but I know that we are meditating the
same old themes that we did when we were ten years
old, only we go more gravely about it.

> —Journal entry, 1849 (correspondence to
> Emerson's 10-year-old daughter, Ellen)

I do not remember ever seeing him laugh outright, but
he was ever ready to smile at anything that pleased
him; and I never knew him to betray any tender emotion except on one occasion, when he was narrating to
me the death of his only brother, John Thoreau, from
lockjaw, strong symptoms of which, from his sympathy
with the sufferer, he himself experienced. At this time
his voice was choked, and he shed tears, and went to
the door for air. The subject was of course dropped,
and never recurred to again.

> —Daniel Ricketson, as quoted in the book
> *Thoreau as Seen by His Contemporaries*
> by Walter Harding

Is not disease the rule of existence? There is not a
lily pad floating on the river but has been riddled by
insects. Almost every shrub and tree has its gall, of-
tentimes esteemed its chief ornament and hardly to be
distinguished from the fruit. If misery loves company,
misery has company enough. Now, at midsummer,
find me a perfect leaf or fruit.

> —Journal entry, 1851

It appears to me that at a very early age the mind of man, perhaps at the same time with his body, ceases to be elastic. His intellectual power becomes something defined and limited. He does not think expansively, as he would stretch himself in his growing days. What was flexible sap hardens into heartwood, and there is no further change. In the season of youth, methinks, man is capable of intellectual effort and performance which surpass all rules and bounds; as the youth lays out his whole strength without fear or prudence and does not feel his limits. It is the transition from poetry to prose. The young man can run and leap; he has not learned exactly how far, he knows no limits. The grown man does not exceed his daily labor. He has no strength to waste.

—Journal entry, 1852

The youth gets together his materials to build a bridge to the moon, or, perchance, a palace or temple on the earth, and, at length, the middle-aged man concludes to build a woodshed with them.

—Journal entry, 1852

We begin to die, not in our senses or extremities, but in our divine faculties. Our members may be sound, our sight and hearing perfect, but our genius and imagination betray signs of decay. You tell me that you are growing old and are troubled to see without glasses, but this is unimportant if the divine faculty of the seer shows no signs of decay.

—Journal entry, 1854

Consider what a vast crop is thus annually shed upon the earth. This, more than any mere grain or seed, is

the great harvest of the year. This annual decay and death, this dying by inches, before the whole tree at last lies down and turns to soil. As trees shed their leaves, so deer their horns, and men their hair or nails. The year's great crop. I am more interested in it than in the English grass alone or in the corn. It prepares the virgin mold for future cornfields on which the earth fattens. They teach us how to die.

—Journal entry, 1853

I perceive that we partially die ourselves through sympathy at the death of each of our friends or near relatives. Each such experience is an assault on our vital force. It becomes a source of wonder that they who have lost many friends still live. After long watching around the sickbed of a friend, we, too, partially give up the ghost with him, and are the less to be identified with this state of things.

—Journal entry, 1859

The story goes that on his deathbed Thoreau was asked if he had made peace with God. He replied, "I was not aware that we had ever quarreled." When asked if he was ready for the next world, he said, "One world at a time."

Human Society and Culture

Society is a contrived reality. Expediency is valued; truth is not.

Thoreau believed that humanity had embarked upon a path that could only lead to unhappiness, a lack of satisfaction in life, that would be ultimately self-destructive.

Disobedience is the true foundation of liberty. The obedient must be slaves.

The greatest compliment that was ever paid me was when one asked me what I thought, and attended to my answer.

But lo! Men have become the tools of their tools.

Where there is a lull in truth an institution springs up.

The words of some men are thrown forcibly against you and adhere like burrs.

It requires nothing less than a chivalric feeling to sustain a conversation with a lady.

Wherever a man goes men will pursue and paw him with their dirty institutions.
 —Journal entry, 1850

Pile up your books, the records of sadness, your saws and your laws. Nature is glad outside, and her merry worms within will ere long topple them down. There is a prairie beyond your laws. Nature is a prairie for outlaws. There are two worlds, the post office and nature. I know them both. I continually forget mankind and their institutions, as I do a bank.
 —Journal entry, 1853

There is a solid bottom everywhere. We read that the traveler asked the boy if the swamp before him had a hard bottom. The boy replied that it had. But presently the traveler's horse sank in up to the girths, and he observed to the boy, "I thought you said that this bog had a hard bottom." "So it has," answered the latter, "but you have not got halfway to it yet." So it is with the bogs and quicksands of society; but he is an old boy that knows it. Only what is thought, said, or done at a certain rare coincidence is good. I would not be one of those who will foolishly drive a nail into mere lath and plastering; such a deed would keep me awake nights. Give me a hammer, and let me feel for the furring. Do not depend on the putty. Drive a nail home and clinch it so faithfully that you can wake up in the night and think of your work with satisfaction—a work at which you would not be ashamed to invoke the Muse. So will help you God, and so only. Every nail driven should be as another rivet in the machine of the universe, you carrying on the work.

Rather than love, than money, than fame, give me truth.

—*Walden*, "Conclusion," 1854

My advice to the State is simply this: to dissolve her union with the slaveholder instantly. She can find no respectable law or precedent which sanctions its continuance. And to each inhabitant of Massachusetts, to dissolve his union with the State, as long as she hesitates to do her duty.

—Journal entry, 1854

Who can be serene in a country where both rulers and ruled are without principle? The remembrance of the baseness of politicians spoils my walks. My thoughts are murder to the State; I endeavor in vain to observe nature; my thoughts involuntarily go plotting against the State. I trust that all just men will conspire.

—Journal entry, 1854

I sometimes seem to myself to owe all my little success, all for which men commend me, to my vices. I am perhaps more willful than others and make enormous sacrifices, even of others' happiness, it may be, to gain my ends. It would seem even as if nothing good could be accomplished without some vice to aid in it.

—Journal entry, 1854

I affect what would commonly be called a mean and miserable way of living. I thoroughly sympathize with all savages and gypsies in so far as they merely assert the original right of man to the productions of Nature and a place in her. The Irishman moves into the town, sets up a shanty on the railroad land, and then gleans the dead wood from the neighboring forest, which would never get to market. But the so-called owner forbids it and complains of him as a trespasser. The highest law gives a thing to him who can use it.

—Journal entry, 1855

I see the old pale-faced farmer out again on his sled for the five-thousandth time—Cyrus Hubbard, a man of certain New England probity and worth, immortal and natural, like a natural product, like the sweetness of a nut, like the toughness of hickory. He, too, is a redeemer for me. How superior actually to the faith he professes! He is not an office-seeker. What an institution, what a revelation is a man! We are wont foolishly to think that the creed which a man professes is more significant than the fact he is. It matters not how hard the conditions seemed, how hard the world, for a man is a prevalent force and a new law himself. He is a system whose law is to be observed. The old farmer condescends to countenance still this nature and order of things. It is a great encouragement that an honest man makes this world his abode . . . Moderate, natural, true, as if he were made of earth, stone, wood, snow. I thus meet in this universe kindred of mine, composed of these elements. I see men like frogs; their peeping I partially understand.

—Journal entry, December 1, 1856

It galls me to listen to the remarks of craven-hearted neighbors who speak disparagingly of [John] Brown because he resorted to violence, resisted the government, threw his life away!—what way have they thrown their lives, pray?—neighbors who would praise a man for attacking singly an ordinary band of thieves or murderers. Such minds are not equal to the occasion. They preserve the so-called peace of their community by deeds of petty violence every day. Look at the policeman's billy and handcuffs! Look at the jail! Look at the gallows! Look at the chaplain of the regiment! We are hoping only to live safely on the outskirts of *this* provisional army. So they defend themselves and our hen roosts, and maintain slavery.

—Journal entry, 1859

The Art of Living a Meaningful Life

Elements of a quality life: live simply, do quality work that is not rushed, avoid waste, live below your means, and keep a reserve. Set aside a substantial portion of your time for leisure.

Be not simply good; be good for something.

I cannot tell you what I am, more than a ray of the summer's sun. What I am I am, and say not. Being is the great explainer.

Time: If not aware of its inestimable value, sell it to the highest bidder for cash, and always be cheated. No one but a fool ever sold more of his time than he had to.

Pursue some path, however narrow and crooked, in which you can walk with love and reverence. Wherever a man separates from the multitude and goes his own way, there is a fork in the road, though the travelers along the highway see only a gap in the paling.

Goodness is the only investment that never fails.

There is no more fatal blunderer than he who consumes the greater part of his life getting his living.

A man should greet each dawn joyfully and always consider the nights too long an absenting from one's work.
—Thoreau as quoted by Sigurd Olson in his diary

Most men lead lives of quiet desperation and go to the grave with the song still in them.

As a single footstep will not make a path on the earth, so a single thought will not make a pathway in the mind. To make a deep physical path, we walk again and again. To make a deep mental path, we must think over and over the kind of thoughts we wish to dominate our lives.

What the banker sighs for, the meanest clown may have: leisure and a quiet mind.

It is not enough to be industrious; so are the ants. What are you industrious about?

I say, beware of all enterprises that require new clothes, and not rather a new wearer of clothes.

We should come home from adventures, and perils, and discoveries every day with new experience and character.

A truly good book teaches me better than to read it. I must soon lay it down, and commence living on its hint. What I began by reading, I must finish by acting.

Thoreau and the Art of Life

One is wise to cultivate the tree that bears fruit in our soul.

The most amazing thing about the pyramids of Egypt is that enough people could be found degraded enough to build them, when they should have taken that ambitious booby, the Pharaoh, and drowned him in the Nile.

—Thoreau, as quoted by Edward Abbey

The order of things should be somewhat reverse: the seventh should be man's day of toil, wherein to earn his living by the sweat of his brow; and the other six his Sabbath of the affections and the soul, in which to range his widespread garden.

—From Thoreau's speech given at Harvard, 1837, when he was 20 years of age

The really efficient laborer will be found not to crowd his day with work, but will saunter to his task surrounded by a wide halo of ease and leisure.

—Journal entry, 1842

Pursue, keep up with, circle round and round your life, as a dog does his master's chaise. Do what you love. Know your own bone, gnaw at it, bury it, unearth it, and gnaw it still.

—Letter to Harrison Blake, March 1848

As for doing good . . . I have tried it fairly, and strange as it may seem, am satisfied that it does not agree with my constitution. . . . I came into this world not

chiefly to make this a good place to be in, but to live in it, be it good or bad.

—*Civil Disobedience*, 1849

The perception of beauty is a moral test.

—Journal entry, September 1850

With all your science can you tell how it is, and whence it is, that light comes into the soul?

—Journal entry, 1851

I saw an organ-grinder this morning before a rich man's house, thrilling the street with harmony, loosening the very paving stones and tearing the routine of life to rags and tatters, when the lady of the house shoved up a window and in a semiphilanthropic tone inquired if he wanted anything to eat. But he, very properly it seemed to me, kept on grinding and paid no attention to her question, feeding her ears with melody unasked for. So the world shoves up its window and interrogates the poet, and sets him to gauging ale casks in return. It seemed to me that the music suggested that the recompense should be as fine as the gift. It would be much nobler to enjoy the music, though you paid no money for it, than to presume always a beggarly relation. It is after all, perhaps, the best instrumental music that we have.

—Journal entry, May 27, 1851

I am reminded of Haydon the painter's experience when he went about painting the nobility. I go about to the houses of the farmers and squires in like manner. This is my portrait painting—when I would fain be employed on higher subjects. I have offered myself much more earnestly as a lecturer than a surveyor. Yet I do not get any employment as a lecturer; was not invited to lecture once last winter, and only once (without pay) this winter. But I can get surveying enough, which a hundred others in this county can do as well as I, though it is not boasting much to say that a hundred others in New England cannot lecture as well as I on my themes. But they who do not make the highest demand on you shall rue it. It is because they make a low demand on themselves. All the while that they use only your humbler faculties, your higher unemployed faculties, like an invisible scimitar, are cutting them in twain. Woe be to the generation that

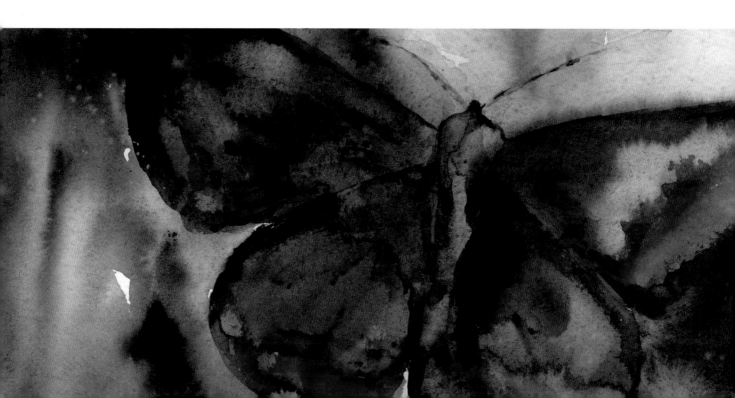

lets any higher faculty in its midst go unemployed! That is to deny God and know him not, and he, accordingly, will know not of them.

—Journal entry, December 22, 1853

The great art of life is how to turn the surplus life of the soul into life for the body—so that life be not a failure. . . . If I should sell both my forenoons and afternoons to society, as most appear to do, I am sure that for me there would be nothing left worth living for. I trust that I shall never thus sell my birthright for a mess of pottage. I wish to suggest that a man may be very industrious, and yet not spend his time well. There is no more fatal blunderer than he who consumes the greater part of his life getting his living. All great enterprises are self-supporting. The poet, for instance, must sustain his body by his poetry, as a steam planing mill feeds its boilers with the shavings it makes. You must get your living by loving.

—Journal entry, March 13, 1853

I learned this, at least, by my experiment: that if one advances confidently in the direction of his dreams, and endeavors to live the life which he has imagined, he will meet with a success unexpected in common

hours. He will put some things behind, will pass an invisible boundary; new, universal, and more liberal laws will begin to establish themselves around and within him; or the old laws be expanded, and interpreted in his favor in a more liberal sense, and he will live with the license of a higher order of beings. In proportion as he simplifies his life, the laws of the universe will appear less complex, and solitude will not be solitude, nor poverty poverty, nor weakness weakness. If you have built castles in the air, your work need not be lost; that is where they should be. Now put the foundations under them.

—*Walden,* "Conclusion," 1854

The cost of a thing is the amount of what I will call life which is required to be exchanged for it, immediately or in the long run.

—*Walden*, "Economy," 1854

One young man of my acquaintance, who has inherited some acres, told me that he thought he should live as I did, if he had the means. I would not have anyone adopt my mode of living on any account; for, besides that before he has fairly learned it I may have found out another for myself, I desire that there may be as many different persons in the world as possible; but I would have each one be very careful to find out and pursue his own way, and not his father's or his mother's or his neighbor's instead. The youth may build or plant or sail, only let him not be hindered from doing that which he tells me he would like to do. . . . We may not arrive at our port within a calculable period, but we would preserve the true course.

—*Walden*, "Economy," 1854

I see young men, my townsmen, whose misfortune it is to have inherited farms, houses, barns, cattle, and farming tools; for these are more easily acquired than gotten rid of.

—*Walden*, "Economy," 1854

If a man does not keep pace with his companions, perhaps it is because he hears a different drummer. Let him step to the music which he hears, however measured or far away.

—*Walden*, "Conclusion," 1854

The life in us is like the water in the river. It may rise this year higher than man has ever known it, and flood the parched uplands; even this may be the eventful year, which will drown out all our muskrats. It was not always dry land where we dwell. I see far

Thoreau and the Art of Life

inland the banks which the stream anciently washed, before science began to record its freshets.

Everyone has heard the story which has gone the rounds of New England, of a strong and beautiful bug which came out of the dry leaf of an old table of apple-tree wood, which had stood in a farmer's kitchen for sixty years, first in Connecticut, and afterwards in Massachusetts, from an egg deposited in the living tree many years earlier still, as appeared by counting the annual layers beyond it; which was heard gnawing out for several weeks, hatched perchance by the heat of an urn. Who does not feel his faith in a resurrection and immortality strengthened by hearing of this? Who knows what beautiful and winged life, whose egg had been buried for ages under many concentric layers of woodenness in the dead dry life of society, deposited at first in the alburnum of the green and living tree, which has been gradually converted into the semblance of its well seasoned tomb—heard perchance gnawing out now for years by the astonished family of man, as they sat round the festive board—may unexpectedly come forth from amidst society's most trivial and handseled furniture, to enjoy its perfect summer life at last!

—*Walden*, "Conclusion," 1854

Give me the poverty that enjoys true wealth.

—*Walden*, "The Ponds," 1854

The true harvest of my life is intangible—a little star dust caught, a portion of the rainbow I have clutched.

—*Walden*, "The Ponds," 1854

What old people say you cannot do, you try and find that you can. Old deeds for old people, and new deeds for new.

—*Walden*, "Economy," 1854

Why do you stay here and live this mean toiling life when a glorious existence is possible for you? These same stars twinkle over other fields than these.

—*Walden*, "The Ponds," 1854

I went to the woods because I wished to live deliberately, to front only the essential facts of life, and see if I could not learn what it had to teach, and not, when I came to die, discover that I had not lived. I did not wish to live what was not life, living is so dear, nor did I wish to practice resignation, unless it was quite necessary. I wanted to live deep and suck out all the marrow of life, to live so sturdily and Spartan-like as to put to rout all that was not life, to cut a broad swath and shave close, to drive life into a corner, and reduce it to its lowest terms, and, if it proved to be mean, why then to get the whole and genuine meanness of

it, and publish its meanness to the world; or if it were sublime, to know it by experience, and be able to give a true account of it in my next excursion.

—*Walden*, "Where I Lived, and What I Lived For," 1854

Most men, even in this comparatively free country, through mere ignorance and mistake, are so occupied with the factitious cares and superfluously coarse labors of life that its finer fruits cannot be plucked by them. . . . Actually, the laboring man has not leisure for a true integrity day by day; he cannot afford to sustain the manliest relations to me; his labor would be depreciated in the marketplace. He has no time to be anything but a machine.

—*Walden*, "Economy," 1854

Some of you, we all know, are poor, find it hard to live, are sometimes, as it were, gasping for breath. I have no doubt that some of you who read this book are unable to pay for all the dinners which you have actually eaten, or for the coats and shoes which are fast wearing or are already worn out, and have come to this page to spend borrowed or stolen time, robbing your creditors of an hour. It is very evident what mean and sneaking lives many of you live, for my sight has been whetted by experience; always on the limits, trying to get into

business and trying to get out of debt . . . always promising to pay, promising to pay, tomorrow, and dying today, insolvent; seeking to curry favor, to get custom, by how many modes, only not state-prison offenses; lying, flattering, voting, contracting yourselves into a nutshell of civility, or dilating into an atmosphere of thin and vaporous generosity, that you may persuade your neighbor to let you make his shoes, or his hat, or his coat, or his carriage, or import his groceries for him; making yourselves sick, that you may lay up something against a sick day, something to be tucked away in an old chest, or more safely, in the brick bank; no matter where, no matter how much or how little.

—*Walden*, "Economy," 1854

Some, not wise, go to the other side of the globe, to barbarous and unhealthy regions, devote themselves to trade for ten or twenty years, in order that they may live—that is, keep comfortably warm—and die in New England at last.

—*Walden*, "Economy," 1854

Most of the luxuries, and many of the so-called comforts of life, are not only not indispensable, but positive hindrances to the elevation of mankind.

—*Walden*, "Economy," 1854

Remember thy creator in the days of thy youth.
Rise free from care before the dawn, and seek
  adventures.
Let the noon find thee by other lakes,
and the night overtake thee everywhere at home.
There are no larger fields than these,
no worthier games than may here be played.
Grow wild according to thy nature,
like these sedges and brakes,
which will never become English hay.
Let the thunder rumble;
what if it threaten ruin to farmers' crops?
That is not its errand to thee.
Take shelter under the cloud,
while they flee to carts and sheds.
Let not to get a living be thy trade, but thy sport.
Enjoy the land, but own it not.
Through want of enterprise and faith men are where
  they are,
buying and selling, and spending their lives like serfs.

     —*Walden*, "Baker Farm," 1854

When a man is warmed by the several modes which
I have described, what does he want next? Surely not
more warmth of the same kind, as more and richer
food, larger and more splendid houses, finer and more
abundant clothing, more numerous and incessant and
hotter fires, and the like. When he has obtained those
things which are necessary to life, there is another
alternative than to obtain the superfluities; and that is,
to adventure on life now, his vacation from humbler
toil having commenced.

     —*Walden*, "Economy," 1854

For more than five years, I maintained myself this
solely by the labor of my hands, and I found, that by
working about six weeks a year, I could meet all the
expenses of living.

     —*Walden*, "Economy," 1854

Some are "industrious," and appear to love labor for
its own sake, or perhaps because it keeps them out
of worse mischief; to such I have at present nothing
to say. Those who would not know what to do with
more leisure than they now enjoy, I might advise to
work twice as hard as they do—work till they pay for
themselves, and get their free papers. For myself I
have found that the occupation of a day laborer was
the most independent of any, especially as it required
only thirty or forty days in a year to support one. The
laborer's day ends with the going down of the sun, and
he is then free to devote himself to his chosen pursuit,
independent of his labor; but his employer, who
speculates from month to month, has no respite from
one end of the year to another.

     —*Walden*, "Economy," 1854

In short, I am convinced, both by faith and experience, that to maintain one's self on this earth is not
a hardship but a pastime, if we will live simply and
wisely; as the pursuits of the simpler nations are still

the sports of the more artificial. It is not necessary that a man should earn his living by the sweat of his brow, unless he sweats easier than I do.

—*Walden*, "Economy," 1854

The true poet will ever live aloof from society, wild to it, as the finest singer is the wood thrush, a forest bird.

—Journal entry, 1854

After lecturing twice this winter I feel that I am in danger of cheapening myself by trying to become a successful lecturer, i.e., to interest my audiences. I am disappointed to find that most that I am and value myself for is lost, or worse than lost, on my audience.

I fail to get even the attention of the mass. I should suit them better if I suited myself less. I feel that the public demands an average man—average thoughts and manners—not originality, nor even absolute excellence. You cannot interest them except as you are like them and sympathize with them. I would rather that my audience come to me than that I should go to them, and so they be sifted; i.e., I would rather write books than lectures. That is fine, this course. To read to a promiscuous audience who are at your mercy the fine thoughts you solaced yourself with far away is as violent as to fatten geese by cramming, and in this case they do not get fatter.

—Journal entry, December 6, 1854

Many will complain of my lectures that they are transcendental. "Can't understand them." "Would you have us return to the savage state?" etc., etc. A criticism true enough, it may be, from their point of view. But the fact is, the earnest lecturer can speak only to his like, and the adapting of himself to his audience is a mere compliment which he pays them. If you wish to know how I think, you must endeavor to put yourself in my place. If you wish me to speak as if I were you, that is another affair.

—Journal entry, 1855

It is interesting to me to talk with Rice, he lives so thoroughly and satisfactorily to himself. He has learned that rare art of living, the very elements of which most professors do not know. His life has been not a failure but a success. Seeing me going to sharpen some plane irons, and hearing me complain of the want of tools, he said that I ought to have a chest of tools. But I said it was not worth the while. I should not use them enough to pay for them. "You would use them more, if you had them," said he. "When I came to do a piece of work I used to find commonly that I wanted a certain tool, and I made it as rule first always to make that tool. I have spent as much as $3,000 thus on my tools."

Comparatively speaking, his life is a success; not such a failure as most men's. He gets more out of any enterprise than his neighbors, for he helps himself more and hires less. Whatever pleasure there is in it he enjoys. By good sense and calculation he has become rich and has invested his property well, yet practices a fair and neat economy, dwells not in untidy luxury. It costs him less to live, and he gets more out of life, than others. To get his living, or keep it, is not a hasty or disagreeable toil. He works slowly but surely, enjoying the sweet of it. He buys a piece of meadow at a profitable rate, works at it in pleasant weather, he and his son, when they are inclined, goes a-fishing or a-bee-hunting, or a-rifle-shooting quite as often, and thus the meadow gets redeemed, and potatoes get planted, perchance, and he is very sure to have a good crop stored in his cellar in the fall, and some to sell. He always has the best of potatoes there. In the same spirit in which he and his son tackle up their dobbin (he never keeps a fast horse) and go a-spearing or a-fishing through the ice, they also tackle up and go to their Sudbury farm to hoe or harvest a little, and when they return they bring home a load of stumps in their hay rigging, which impede their labors, but, perchance, supply them with their winter wood. All the woodchucks they shoot or trap in the bean field are brought home also. And thus their life is a long sport and they know not what hard times are.

—Journal entry, November 17, 1855

In my experience I have found nothing so truly impoverishing as what is called wealth, i.e., the command of greater means than you had before possessed, though comparatively few and slight still, for you thus inevitably acquire a more expensive habit of living, and even the very same necessaries and comforts cost you more than they once did. Instead of gaining, you have lost some independence, and if your income should be suddenly lessened, you would find yourself poor, though possessed of the same means which once made you rich. Within the last five years I have had the command of a little more money than in the previous five years, for I have sold some books and some lectures; yet I have not been a whit better fed or clothed or warmed or sheltered, not a whit richer, except that I have been less concerned and, to balance it, I feel now that there is a possibility of failure. Who knows but I *may* come upon the town, if, as is likely, the public want no more of my books, or lectures (which last is already the case)? Before, I was much likelier to take the town upon my shoulders. That is, I have lost some of my independence on them, when they would say

that I had gained an independence. If you wish to give a man a sense of poverty, give him a thousand dollars. The next hundred dollars he gets will not be worth more than ten that he used to get. Have pity on him; withhold your gifts.

—Journal entry, January 20, 1856

Our employment generally is tinkering, mending the old worn-out teapot of society. Our stock in trade is solder. Better for me, says my genius, to go cranberrying this afternoon.

—Journal entry, August 30, 1856

I see that my neighbors look with compassion on me, that they think it is a mean and unfortunate destiny which makes me to walk in these fields and woods so much and sail on this river alone. But so long as I find here the only real elysium, I cannot hesitate in my choice. My work is writing, and I do not hesitate, though I know that no subject is too trivial for me, tried by ordinary standards; for, ye fools, the theme is nothing, the life is everything. All that interests the reader is the depth and intensity of the life excited.

—Journal entry, October 18, 1856

For some years past I have partially offered myself as a lecturer; have been advertised as such [for] several years. Yet I have had but two or three invitations to lecture in a year, and some years none at all. I congratulate myself on having been permitted to stay at home thus, I am so much richer for it. I do not see what I should have got of much value, but money, by going about, but I do see what I should have lost. It seems to me that I have a longer and more liberal lease on life thus. I cannot afford to be telling my experience, especially to those who perhaps will take no interest in it. I wish to

be getting experience. You might as well recommend to a bear to leave his hollow tree in the woods. He would be leaner in the spring than if he had stayed at home and sucked his claws.

—Journal entry, January 11, 1857

Men's minds run so much on work and money that the mass instantly associate all literary labor with a pecuniary reward. They are mainly curious to know how much money the lecturer or author gets for his work. They think that the naturalist takes so much pains to collect plants or animals because he is paid for it.

—Journal entry, 1859

Talk about slavery! It is not the peculiar institution of the South. It exists wherever men are bought and sold, wherever a man allows himself to be made a mere thing or a tool, and surrenders his inalienable rights of reason and conscience. Indeed, this slavery is more complete than that which enslaves the body alone. It exists in the Northern states, and I am reminded by what I find in the newspapers that it exists in Canada. I never yet

met with, or heard of, a judge who was not a slave of this kind, and so the finest and most unfailing weapon of injustice. He fetches a slightly higher price than the black man only because he is a more valuable slave.

—Journal entry, 1860

I rejoice that horses and steers have to be broken before they can be made the slaves of men, and that men themselves have some wild oats still to sow before they become submissive members of society. Undoubtedly all men are not equally fit subjects for civilization; and because the majority, like dogs and sheep, are tame by inherited disposition, this is no reason why the others should have their natures broken that they may be reduced to the same level. Men are in the main alike, but they were made several in order that they might be various. If a low use is to be served, one man will do quite as well as another; if a high one, individual excellence is to be regarded. Any man can stop a hole to keep the wind away, but no other man could serve so rare a use as the author of this illustration did. Confucius says, "The skins of the tiger and the leopard, when they are tanned, are as the skins of the dog and the sheep tanned." But it is not the part of a true culture to tame tigers, any more than it is to make sheep ferocious; and tanning their skins for shoes is not the best use to which they can be put.

—"Walking," a speech Thoreau gave in 1851, published in 1863

Nature and the Human Connection to the Natural World

A close relationship with nature contributes joy and peace to a human life. Simple living enhances our awareness of, and openness to, the beauty of the natural world.

He (HDT) was talking to Mr. Alcott of the wildflowers in Walden woods when, suddenly stopping, he said, "Keep very still and I will show you my family." Stepping quickly outside the cabin door, he gave a low and curious whistle; immediately a woodchuck came running toward him from a nearby burrow. With varying note, yet still low and strange, a pair of gray squirrels were summoned and approached him fearlessly. With still another note, several birds, including two crows, flew toward him, one of the crows nestling upon his shoulder. I remember it was the crow resting close to his head that made the most vivid impression upon me, knowing how fearful of man this bird is. He fed them all from his hand, taking food from his pocket, and petted them gently before our delighted gaze; and then dismissed them by different whistling, always strange and low and short, each little wild thing departing instantly at hearing his special signal.

—Frederick Willis recalling a visit to Walden Pond in July 1847 with the Alcott family

"Henry D. Thoreau—Henry D. Thoreau," jerking out the words with withering contempt. "His name ain't no more Henry D. Thoreau than my name is Henry D. Thoreau. And everybody knows it, and he knows it. His name's *Da*-a-vid Henry and it ain't never been nothing but *Da*-a-vid Henry. And he knows that! Why one morning I went out in my field across there to the river, and there, beside that little old mud pond, was standing *Da*-a-vid Henry, and he wasn't doin' nothin'

but just standin' there—lookin' at that pond, and when I came back at noon, there he was standin' with his hands behind him just lookin' down into that pond, and after dinner when I come back again if there wan't *Da*-a-vid standin' there just like as if he had been there all day, gazin' down into that pond, and I stopped and looked at him and I says, '*Da*-a-vid Henry, what air you a-doin'?' And he didn't turn his head and he didn't look at me. He kept on lookin' down at that pond, and he said, as if he was thinkin' about the stars in the heavens, 'Mr. Murray, I'm a-studyin'—the habits—of the bullfrog!' And there that darned fool had been standin'—the livelong day—*a-studyin'*—the habits—of the *bull*frog!'"

> —Mr. Murray, a local farmer, as quoted in *Thoreau as Seen by His Contemporaries*. Henry David Thoreau was actually baptized David Henry Thoreau. Although he did not legally change his name, he adopted Henry David by personal preference.

One day . . . we children saw Mr. Thoreau standing right down there across the road near the Assabet. He stood very still, and we knew he was watching something in the water. But we knew we must not disturb him, and so we stayed up here in the dooryard. At noontime he was still there, watching something in the water. And he stayed there all afternoon.

At last, though, along about supper time, he came up here to the house. And then we children knew that we'd learn what it was he'd been watching. He'd found a duck that had just hatched out a nest of eggs. She had brought the little ducks down to the water. And Mr. Thoreau had watched all day to see her teach those little ducks about the river.

And while we ate our suppers there in the kitchen, he told us the most wonderful stories you ever heard about those ducks.

—Abby Hosmer, as quoted in *Thoreau as Seen by His Contemporaries*

I have come to believe that most of us have experienced some lonely spot, some private nook, some glen or streamside scene that impressed us so deeply that even today its memory recalls the mood of a lost enchantment. At the age of eighty, my grandmother used to recall with delight a lonely tract she called Beautiful Big South Woods. There, as a girl one spring day, she had seen the whole floor of the woods, acre on acre, carpeted with the blooms of bloodroot and spring beauties and blue and pink hepaticas. She had seen the woods only once but she never forgot it.

When Henry Thoreau was five, his parents, then living in the city of Boston, took him eighteen miles into the country to a woodland scene that he, too, never forgot. It was, he said, one of the earliest scenes stamped on the tablets of his memory. During succeeding years of childhood, that woodland formed the basis of his dreams. The spot to which he had been taken was Walden Pond, near Concord. Twenty-three years later, writing in his cabin on the shores of this same pond, Thoreau noted the unfading impression that fabulous landscape had made and how, even at that early age, he had given preference to this recess—where almost sunshine and shadow were the only inhabitants that varied the scene—over the tumultuous city in which he lived.

—Edwin Way Teale, *The Lost Woods*

You must not know too much or be too precise or scientific about birds and trees and flowers and watercraft; a certain free-margin, and even vagueness—ignorance, credulity—helps your enjoyment of these things.

I love to see anything that implies a simpler mode of life and a greater nearness to the earth.

If a man walks in the woods for love of them half of each day, he is in danger of being regarded as a loafer. But if he spends his days as a speculator, shearing off those woods and making the earth bald before her time, he is deemed an industrious and enterprising citizen.

The setting sun is reflected from the windows of the almshouse as brightly as from the rich man's abode.

My heart leaps into my mouth at the sound of the wind in the woods.

When the question of the protection of birds comes up, the legislatures regard only a low use and never a high use; the best-disposed legislatures employ one, perchance, only to examine their crops and see how many grubs or cherries they contain, and never to study their dispositions, or the beauty of their plumage, or listen and report on the sweetness of their song. The legislature will preserve a bird professedly not because it is a beautiful creature, but because it is a good scavenger or the like. This, at least, is the defense set up. It is as if the question were whether some celebrated singer of the human race—some Jenny Lind or another—did

more harm than good; should be destroyed, or not, and therefore a committee should be appointed, not to listen to her singing at all, but to examine the contents of her stomach and see if she devoured anything which was injurious to the farmers and gardeners, or which they cannot spare.

When a new country like North America is discovered, a few feeble efforts are made to Christianize the natives before they are all exterminated, but they are not found to pay, in any sense. But the energetic traders of the discovering country organize themselves, or rather inevitably crystallize, into a vast rat-catching society, tempt the natives to become mere vermin-hunters and rum-drinkers, reserving half a continent for the field of their labors. Savage meets savage, and the white man's only distinction is that he is chief.

This curious world which we inhabit is more wonderful than it is convenient; more beautiful than it is useful; it is more to be admired and enjoyed than used.

The first really foggy morning. Yet before I rise I hear the song of birds from out it, like the bursting of its bubbles with music, the bead on liquids just uncorked. Their song gilds thus the frostwork of the morning. As if the fog were a great sweet froth on the surface of land and water, whose fixed air escaped, whose bubbles burst with music. The sound of its evaporation, the fixed air of the morning just brought from the cellars of the night escaping. The morning twittering of birds in perfect harmony with it. I came near awaking this morning. I am older than last year; the mornings are further between; the days are fewer. Any

excess—to have drunk too much water, even, the day before—is fatal to the morning's clarity, but in health the sound of a cowbell is celestial music.

The farmer keeps pace with his crops and the revolutions of the seasons, but the merchant with the fluctuations of trade. Observe how differently they walk in the streets.

—Journal entry, 1839

The infinite bustle of Nature on a summer's noon, or her infinite silence of a summer's night, gives utterance to no dogma. They do not say to us even with a seer's assurance, that this or that law is immutable and so ever and only can the universe exist. But they are

the indifferent occasion for all things and the annulment of all laws.

—Journal entry, 1840

Nature will bear the closest inspection. She invites us to lay our eye level with her smallest leaf, and take an insect view of its plain.

—"Natural History of Massachusetts," 1842

What sweet and tender, the most innocent and divinely encouraging society there is in every natural object, and so in universal nature, even for the poor misanthrope and most melancholy man! There can be no really black melancholy to him who lives in the midst of nature and has still his senses. There never was yet such a storm but it was Aeolian music to the innocent ear. Nothing can compel to a vulgar sadness a simple and brave man. While I enjoy the sweet friendship of the seasons I trust that nothing can make life a burden to me. This rain which is now watering my beans and keeping me in the house waters me too. I needed it as much. And what if most are not hoed! Those who send the rain, whom I chiefly respect, will pardon me.

—Journal entry, 1845, while living at
    Walden Pond

Talk of mysteries! Think of our life in nature—daily to be shown matter, to come in contact with it— rocks, trees, wind on our cheeks! the *solid* earth! the *actual* world! the *common sense! Contact! Contact! Who* are we? *Where* are we?

—*The Maine Woods,* "Ktaadn," 1848

Measure your health by your sympathy with morning and spring. If there is no response in you to the awakening of nature—if the prospect of an early morning walk does not banish sleep, if the warble of the first bluebird does not thrill you—know that the morning and spring of your life are past. Thus may you feel your pulse.

—Journal entry, 1850

We yearn to see the mountains daily, as the Israelites yearned for the promised land, and we daily live the fate of Moses, who only looked into the promised land from Pisgah before he died.

—Journal entry, 1851

Nature is reported not by him who goes forth consciously as an observer, but in the fullness of life. To such a one she rushes to make her report. To the full heart she is all but a figure of speech.

—Journal entry, 1852

The thrush alone declares the immortal wealth and vigor that is in the forest. Whenever a man hears it, he is young, and Nature is in her spring. Wherever he hears it, it is a new world and a free country, and the gates of heaven are not shut against him.

—Journal entry, 1852

By my intimacy with nature I find myself withdrawn from man. My interest in the sun and the moon, in the morning and the evening, compels me to solitude.

The grandest picture in the world is the sunset sky. In your higher moods what man is there to meet? You are of necessity isolated. The mind that perceives clearly any natural beauty is in that instant withdrawn from human society. My desire for society is infinitely increased; my fitness for any actual society is diminished.

—Journal entry, July 26, 1852

If I am too cold for human friendship, I trust I shall not soon be too cold for natural influences. It appears to be a law that you cannot have a deep sympathy with both man and nature. Those qualities which bring you near to the one estrange you from the other.

—Journal entry, 1852

Man cannot afford to be a naturalist, to look at Nature directly, but only with the side of his eye. He must look through and beyond her. To look at her is fatal as to look at the head of Medusa. It turns the man of science to stone.

—Journal entry, 1853

How significant that the rich, black mud of our dead stream produces the water lily—out of that fertile slime springs this spotless purity! It is remarkable that those flowers which are most emblematical of purity should grow in the mud.

—Journal entry, 1853

All change is a miracle to contemplate; but it is a miracle which is taking place every instant.

—*Walden,* "Economy," 1854

Nature is full of genius, full of the divinity; so that not a snowflake escapes its fashioning hand.

—*Walden,* "Economy," 1854

Thoreau and the Art of Life

I have just been through the process of killing the cistudo [box tortoise] for the sake of science; but I cannot excuse myself for this murder, and see that such actions are inconsistent with the poetic perception, however they may serve science, and will affect the quality of my observations. I pray that I may walk more innocently and serenely through nature. No reasoning whatever reconciles me to this act. It affects my day injuriously. I have lost some self-respect. I have a murderer's experience in a degree.

—Journal entry, 1854

There is a cool east wind—and has been afternoons for several days—which has produced a very thick haze or a fog. I find a tortoise egg on this peak at least sixty feet above the pond. There is a fine ripple and sparkle on the pond, seen through the mist. But what signifies the beauty of nature when men are base? We walk to lakes to see our serenity reflected in them. When we are not serene, we go not to them. Who can be serene in a country where both rulers and ruled are without principle? The remembrance of the baseness of politicians spoils my walks. My thoughts are murder to the State; I endeavor in vain to observe nature; my thoughts involuntarily go plotting against the State. I trust that all just men will conspire.

—Journal entry, 1854

On the outside all the life of the earth is expressed in the animal or vegetable, but make a deep cut in it and you find it vital; you find in the very sands an anticipation of the vegetable leaf. No wonder, then, that plants grow and spring in it. The atoms have already learned the law. Let a vegetable sap convey it upwards and you have a vegetable leaf. No wonder that the earth expresses itself outwardly in leaves, which labors with the idea thus inwardly. The overhanging leaf sees here its prototype. The earth is pregnant with law.

—Journal entry, 1854

The Earth is not a mere fragment of dead history, a stratum upon stratum like the leaves of a book, to be studied by biologists and antiquarians chiefly, but living poetry like the leaves of a tree, which precede flowers and fruit—not a fossil Earth but a living Earth.

—*Walden*, "Spring," 1854

Winter has come unnoticed by me, I have been so busy writing. This is the life most lead in respect to Nature. How different from my habitual one! It is hasty, coarse, and trivial, as if you were a spindle in a factory. The other is leisurely, fine, and glorious, like a flower. In the first case you are merely getting your living; in the second you live as you go along.

—Journal entry, 1854

Shall I not have intelligence with the earth? Am I not partly leaves and vegetable mold myself?

—*Walden*, "Solitude," 1854

When I look at the stars, nothing which the astronomers have said attaches to them, they are so simple and remote. *Their* knowledge is felt to be all terrestrial and to concern the earth alone. It suggests that the same is the case with every object, however familiar; our so-called knowledge of it is equally vulgar and remote.

—Journal entry, 1854

We need the tonic of wildness, to wade sometimes in marshes where the bittern and the meadow hen lurk, and hear the booming of the snipe; to smell the whispering sedge where only some wilder and more solitary fowl builds her nest, and the mink crawls with its belly close to the ground. At the same time that we are earnest to explore and learn all things, we require that all things be mysterious and unexplorable, that land and sea be infinitely wild, unsurveyed and unfathomed by us because it is unfathomable. We can never have enough of nature. We must be refreshed by the sight of inexhaustible vigor, vast and titanic features, the seacoast with its wrecks, the wilderness with its living and its decaying trees, the thunder cloud, and the rain which lasts three weeks and produces freshets. We need to witness our own limits transgressed, and some life pasturing freely where we never wander.

 —*Walden*, "Spring," 1854

So there is one thought for the field, another for the house. I would have my thoughts, like wild apples, to be food for walkers, and will not warrant them to be palatable if tasted in the house.

 —Journal entry, 1855

If any part of nature excites our pity, it is for ourselves we grieve, for there is eternal health and beauty. We get only transient and partial glimpses of the beauty of the world. Standing at the right angle, we are dazzled by the colors of the rainbow in colorless ice. From the right point of view, every storm and every drop in it is a rainbow. Beauty and music are not mere traits and exceptions. They are the rule and character.

 —Journal entry, 1855

The sun is but a morning star.

 —Journal entry, 1856

The eternity which I detect in Nature I predicate of myself also. How many springs I have had this same experience! I am encouraged, for I recognize this steady persistency and recovery of Nature as a quality of myself.

 —Journal entry, 1856

I hear the hyla [toad] peep faintly several times . . . He is the first of his race to awaken to the new year and pierce the solitudes with his voice. He shall wear the medal for this year. You hear him but you will never find him. He is somewhere down amid the withered sedge and alder bushes there by the water's edge, but where?

 —Journal entry, April 9, 1856

It will take you half a lifetime to find the earliest flower.

—Journal entry, March 26, 1856

It is in vain to dream of a wildness distant from ourselves. There is none such. It is the bog in our brain and bowels, the primitive vigor of Nature in us that inspires that dream. I shall never find in the wilds of Labrador any greater wildness than in some recess in Concord, i.e., than I import into it.

—Journal entry, August 30, 1856

It commonly chances that I make my most interesting botanical discoveries when I [am] in a thrilled and expectant mood, perhaps wading in some remote swamp where I have just found something novel and feel more than usually remote from the town. Or some rare plant which for some reason has occupied a strangely prominent place in my thoughts for some time will present itself. My expectation ripens to discovery. I am prepared for strange things.

—Journal entry, 1856

We must go out and re-ally ourselves to Nature every day. We must make root, send out some little fiber at least, even every winter day. I am sensible that I am imbibing health when I open my mouth to the wind. Staying in the house breeds a sort of insanity always. Every house is in this sense a hospital. A night and a forenoon is as much confinement to those wards as I can stand. I am aware that I recover some sanity which I had lost almost the instant that I come abroad.

—Journal entry, 1856

In our workshops we pride ourselves on discovering a use for what had previously been regarded as waste, but how partial and accidental our economy compared with Nature's. In Nature nothing is wasted. Every decayed leaf and twig and fiber is only the better fitted to serve in some other department, and all   at last are gathered in her compost heap.

—Journal entry, 1856

Does he chiefly own the land who coldly uses it and gets corn and potatoes out of it, or he who loves it and gets inspiration from it? How rarely a man's love for nature becomes a ruling principle with him, like a youth's affection for a maiden, but more enduring! All nature is my bride. That nature which to one is a stark and ghastly solitude is a sweet, tender, and genial society to another.

—Journal entry, 1857

In the streets and in society I am almost invariably cheap and dissipated, my life is unspeakably mean. No amount of gold or respectability would in the least redeem it—dining with the Governor or a member of Congress!! But alone in the distant woods or fields, in unpretending sprout-lands or pastures tracked by rabbits, even in a bleak and, to most, cheerless day, like this, when a villager would be thinking of his inn, I come to myself, I once more feel myself grandly related, and that cold and solitude are friends of mine. I suppose that this value, in my case, is equivalent to what others get by churchgoing and prayer. I come home to my solitary woodland walk as the homesick go home. I

thus dispose of the superfluous and see things as they are, grand and beautiful. I have told many that I walk every day about half the daylight, but I think they do not believe it. I wish to get the Concord, the Massachusetts, the America, out of my head and be sane a part of every day.

—Journal entry, January 1857

What a pitiful business is the fur trade, which has been pursued now for so many ages, for so many years by famous companies which enjoy a profitable monopoly and control a large portion of the earth's surface, unweariedly pursuing and ferreting out small animals by the aid of all the loafing class tempted by rum and money, that you may rob some little fellow creature of its coat to adorn or thicken your own, that you may get a fashionable covering in which to hide your head, or a suitable robe in which to dispense justice to your fellow men! Regarded from the philosopher's point of view, it is precisely on a level with rag and bone picking in the streets of the cities. The Indian led a more respectable life before he was tempted to debase himself so much by the white man. Think how many musquash and weasel skins the Hudson's Bay Company pile up annually in their warehouses, leaving the bare red carcasses on the banks of the streams throughout all British America—and this is it, chiefly, which makes it British America. It is the place where Great Britain goes a-mousing. We have heard much of the wonderful intelligence of the beaver, but that regard for the beaver is all a pretense, and we would give more for a beaver hat than to preserve the intelligence of the whole race of beavers.

—Journal entry, April 8, 1859

The old naturalists were so sensitive and sympathetic to nature that they could be surprised by the ordinary events of life. It was an incessant miracle to them, and therefore gorgons and flying dragons were not incredible to them. The greatest and saddest defect is not incredulity, but our habitual forgetfulness that our science is ignorance.

—Journal entry, March 5, 1860

Thus we behave like oxen in a flower garden. The true fruit of Nature can only be plucked with a delicate hand and a fluttering heart, not bribed by any earthly reward. No hired man can help us to gather this crop.

—Journal entry, 1861

But most men, it seems to me, do not care for Nature and would sell their share in all her beauty, as long as they may live, for a stated sum—many for a glass of rum. Thank God, men cannot as yet fly, and lay waste the sky as well as the earth! We are safe on that side for the present. It is for the very reason that some do not care for those things that we need to continue to protect all from the vandalism of a few.

—Journal entry, 1861

I wish to speak a word for Nature, for absolute freedom and wildness, as contrasted with a freedom and culture merely civil—to regard man as an inhabitant, or a part and parcel of Nature, rather than a member of society. I wish to make an extreme statement, if so I may make an emphatic one, for there are enough champions of civilization: the minister and the school committee and every one of you will take care of that.

—"Walking," 1863

I believe that there is a subtle magnetism in Nature, which, if we unconsciously yield to it, will direct us aright. It is not indifferent to us which way we walk. There is a right way; but we are very liable from heedlessness and stupidity to take the wrong one. We would fain take that walk, never yet taken by us through this actual world, which is perfectly symbolical of the path which we love to travel in the interior and ideal world; and sometimes, no doubt, we find it difficult to choose our direction, because it does not yet exist distinctly in our idea.

—"Walking," 1863

All good things are wild, and free.
    —"Walking," 1863

Generally speaking, a howling wilderness does not howl: it is the imagination of the traveler that does the howling.
    —*The Maine Woods,* "The Allegash and East Branch," 1864

Spiritual Existence in a Spiritual Universe

A spiritual life is a life of calmness, of openness to mystery, beauty, and infinity.

Thoreau was constantly looking for opportunities to hook into the deeper underlying realities around him.

Let nothing come between you and the light.

We shall see but a little way if we require to understand what we see.

What is peculiar in the life of a man consists not in his obedience, but his opposition, to his instincts. In one direction or another he strives to live a supernatural life.

Men are constantly dinging in my ears their fair theories and plausible solutions of the universe, but ever there is no help, and I return again to my shoreless, islandless ocean, and fathom unceasingly for a bottom that will hold an anchor, that it may not drag.

—Journal entry, 1838

I tread in the tracks of the fox which has gone before me by some hours, or which perhaps I have started, with such a tiptoe of expectation as if I were on the trail of the Spirit itself which resides in these woods, and expected soon to catch it in its lair.

—Journal entry, 1841

The great God is very calm withal. How superfluous is any excitement in his creatures! He listens equally to the prayers of the believer and the unbeliever. The moods of man should unfold and alternate as gradually and placidly as those of nature. The sun shines for aye! The sudden revolutions of these times and this generation have acquired a very exaggerated importance. They do not interest me much, for they are not in harmony with the longer periods of nature. The present, in any aspect in which it can be presented to the smallest audience, is always mean. God does not sympathize with the popular movements.

—Journal entry, 1842

I find an instinct in me conducting to a mystic spiritual life, and also another to a primitive savage life.

Toward evening, as the world waxes darker, I am permitted to see the woodchuck stealing across my path, and tempted to seize and devour it. The wildest, most desolate scenes are strangely familiar to me.

—Journal entry, 1845

I do not prefer one religion or philosophy to another. I have no sympathy with the bigotry and ignorance which make transient and partial and puerile distinctions between one man's faith or form of faith and another's—as Christian and heathen. I pray to be delivered from narrowness, partiality, exaggeration, bigotry. To the philosopher all sects, all nations, are alike. I like Brahma, Hari, Buddha, the Great Spirit, as well as God.

—Journal entry, 1850

What shall we do with a man who is afraid of the woods, their solitude and darkness? What salvation is there for him? God is silent and mysterious.

—Journal entry, 1850

Nothing is so much to be feared as fear. Atheism may comparatively be popular with God himself.

—Journal entry, 1851

The gods can never afford to leave a man in the world who is privy to any of their secrets. They cannot have a spy here. They will at once send him packing. How can you walk on ground when you see through it?

—Journal entry, 1852

I do not value any view of the universe into which man and the institutions of man enter very largely and absorb much of the attention. Man is but the place where I stand; and the prospect hence is infinite.

—Journal entry, 1852

Sometimes, after staying in a village parlor till the family had all retired, I have returned to the woods, and, partly with a view to the next day's dinner, spent the hours of midnight fishing from a boat by moonlight, serenaded by owls and foxes, and hearing, from time to time, the creaking note of some unknown bird close at hand. These experiences were very memorable and valuable to me—anchored in forty feet of water, and twenty or thirty rods from the shore, surrounded sometimes by thousands of small perch and shiners, dimpling the surface with their tails in the moonlight, communicating by a long flaxen line with mysterious nocturnal fishes which had their dwelling forty feet below, or sometimes dragging sixty feet of line about the pond as I drifted in the gentle night breeze, now and then feeling a slight vibration along it, indicative of some life prowling about its extremity, of dull uncertain blundering purpose there, and slow to make up its mind. At length you slowly raise, pulling hand over hand, some horned pout squeaking and squirming to the upper air. It was very queer, especially in dark nights, when your thoughts had wandered to vast and cosmogonal themes in other spheres, to feel this faint jerk, which came to interrupt your dreams and link you to Nature again. It seemed as if I might next cast my line upward into the air, as well as downward into this element which was scarcely more dense. Thus I caught two fishes as it were with one hook.

—*Walden*, "The Ponds," 1854

By closing the eyes and slumbering and consenting to be deceived by shows, men establish and confirm their daily life of routine and habit everywhere, which still is built on purely illusory foundations. . . . I have read in a Hindu book, that "there was a king's son, who, being expelled in infancy from his native city, was brought up by a forester, and, growing to maturity in that state, imagined himself to belong to the barbarous race with which he lived. One of his father's ministers having discovered him, revealed to him what he was, and the misconception of his character was removed, and he knew himself to be a prince. So soul," continues the Hindu philosopher, "from the circumstances in which it is placed, mistakes its own character, until the truth is revealed to it by some holy teacher, and then it knows itself to be *Brahme.*" I perceive that we inhabitants of New England live this mean life that we do because our vision does not penetrate the surface of things.

—*Walden*, "Where I Lived, and What I Lived For," 1854

In eternity there is indeed something true and sublime. But all these times and places and occasions are now and here. God himself culminates in the present moment and will never be more divine in the lapse of the ages. Time is but a stream I go a-fishing in. I drink at it, but when I drink I see the sandy bottom and detect how shallow it is. Its thin current slides away but eternity remains.

—*Walden*, "Where I Lived, and What I Lived For," 1854

I go across Walden. My shadow is very blue. It is especially blue when there is a bright sunlight on pure white snow. It suggests that there may be something divine, something celestial, in me.

—Journal entry, 1855

I see that men may be well-mannered or conventionally polite toward men, but skeptical toward God.

—Journal entry, 1857

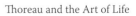

Thoreau and the Art of Life

Walking

Long, frequent walks in the woods bring peace and serenity to a human life.

Long walks in the woods were at the center of Thoreau's relationship with nature, with his work, and with himself. They brought peace and serenity to his life, and deepened his connection to the many things that meant a lot to him, but that he could not understand or explain.

I frequently tramped eight or ten miles through the deepest snow to keep an appointment with a beech tree, or a yellow birch, or an old acquaintance among the pines.

For many years I was a self-appointed inspector of snowstorms and rainstorms, and did my duty faithfully; surveyor, if not of highways, then of forest paths and all across lot routes, keeping them open, and ravines bridged and passable at all seasons, where the public heel had testified to their utility.

It is a great art to saunter.

It is a certain fairyland where we live. You may walk out in any direction over the Earth's surface, lifting your horizon, and everywhere your path, climbing the convexity of the globe, leads you between heaven and Earth, not away from the light of the sun and stars and the habitations of men. I wonder that I ever get five miles on my way, the walk is so crowded with events and phenomena. How many questions there are which I have not put to its inhabitants.

—Journal entry, June 7, 1851

Now I yearn for one of those old, meandering, dry uninhabited roads, which lead away from towns, which lead us away from temptation, which conduct to the outside of Earth, over its uppermost crust; where you may forget in what country you are traveling; where no farmer can complain that you are treading down his grass, no gentleman who has recently constructed a seat in the country that you are trespassing; on which you can go off at half cock and wave adieu to the village; along which you may travel like a pilgrim, going nowhither; where travelers are not too often to be met; where my spirit is free; where the walls and fences are not cared for; where your head is more in heaven than your feet are on earth; which have long reaches where

you can see the approaching traveler half a mile off
and be prepared for him; not so luxuriant a soil as to
attract men; some root and stump fences which do
not need attention; where travelers have no occasion
to stop, but pass along and leave you to your thoughts;
where it makes no odds which way you face, whether
you are going or coming, whether it is morning or
evening, mid-noon or midnight; where earth is cheap
enough by being public; where you can walk and think
with least obstruction, where you can pace when your
breast is full, and cherish your moodiness; where you
are not in false relations with men, are not dining nor
conversing with them; by which you may go to the ut-
termost parts of the earth.

It is wide enough, wide as the thoughts it allows to
visit you. Sometimes it is some particular half-dozen
rods which I wish to find myself pacing over, as where
certain airs blow; then my life will come to me, methinks; like a hunter I walk in wait for it.

When I am against this bare promontory of
a huckleberry hill, then forsooth my thoughts will
expand. Is it some influence, as a vapor which exhales
from the ground, or something in the gales which blow
there, or in all things there brought together agreeably
to my spirit? The walls must not be too high, imprisoning me, but low, with numerous gaps. The trees must
not be too numerous, nor the hills too near, bounding
the view, nor the soil too rich, attracting the attention

to the earth. It must simply be the way and the life—a way that was never known to be repaired, nor to need repair, within the memory of the oldest inhabitant. I cannot walk habitually in those ways that are liable to be mended; for sure it was the devil only that wore them. Never by the heel of thinkers (of thought) were they worn; the zephyrs could repair that damage.

The saunterer wears out no road, even though he travel on it, and therefore should pay no highway, or rather *low* way, tax. He may be taxed to construct a higher way than men travel. A way which no geese defile, nor hiss along it, but only sometimes their wild brethren fly far overhead; which the kingbird and the swallow twitter over, and the song sparrow sings on its rails; where the small red butterfly is at home on the yarrow, and no boys threaten it with imprisoning hat. There I can walk and stalk and pace and plod. Which nobody but Jonas Potter travels beside me; where no cow but his is tempted to linger for the herbage by its side; where the guide-board is fallen, and now the hand points to heaven significantly—to a Sudbury and Marlborough in the skies.

That's a road I can travel, that the particular Sudbury I am bound for, six miles an hour, or two, as you please; and few there be that enter thereon. There I can walk, and recover the lost child that I am without any ringing of a bell.

—Journal entry, July 21, 1851, 8 AM

Even in remotest woods the trivial noon has its rule and its limit. When the chaste and pensive eve draws on, suddenly the walker begins to reflect.

—Journal entry, 1853

When, after feeling dissatisfied with my life, I aspire to something better, am more scrupulous, more reserved and continent, as if expecting somewhat, suddenly I find myself full of life as a nut of meat—am overflowing with a quiet, gentle mirthfulness. I think of myself, I must attend to my diet; I must get up earlier and take

a morning walk; I must have done with luxuries and devote myself to my muse. So I dam up my stream, and my waters gather to a head. I am freighted with thought.

—Journal entry, October 26, 1853

I find it good to be out this still, dark, mizzling afternoon; my walk or voyage is more suggestive and profitable than in bright weather. The view is contracted by the misty rain, the water is perfectly smooth, and the stillness is favorable to reflection. I am more open to impressions, more sensitive (not calloused or indurated by sun and wind), as if in a chamber still. My thoughts are concentrated; I am all compact. The solitude is real, too, for the weather keeps other men at home. This mist is like a roof and walls over and around, and I walk with a domestic feeling. The sound of a wagon going over an unseen bridge is louder than ever, and so of other sounds. I am *compelled* to look at near objects. All things have a soothing effect; the very clouds and mists brood over me. My power of observation and contemplation is much increased. My attention does not wander. The world and my life are simplified. What now of Europe and Asia?

—Journal entry, November 7, 1855

Take long walks in stormy weather or through deep snows in the fields and woods, if you would keep your spirits up. Deal with brute nature. Be cold and hungry and weary.

—Journal entry, 1856

Wisdom, Truth, Solitude, Simplicity

Wisdom and simplicity are closely related.

According to everything we know, Thoreau was unsusceptible to temptation. He believed that wisdom and simplicity were closely related. He declined invitations to dinner parties, avoided alcohol because it interfered with his taste for water, and when asked what food he liked best, he responded, "The nearest." He seems to have distrusted the pleasures of intimate sensuality.

When we are unhurried and wise, we perceive that only great and worthy things have any permanent and absolute existence, that petty fears and petty pleasures are but the shadow of the reality.

All good things are cheap: all bad are very dear.

It is a characteristic of wisdom not to do desperate things.

Every man looks at his woodpile with a kind of affection.

The knowledge of an unlearned man is living and luxuriant like a forest, but covered with mosses and lichens and for the most part inaccessible and going to waste; the knowledge of the man of science is like timber collected in yards for public works, which still supports a green sprout here and there, but even this is liable to dry rot.

Truths and roses have thorns about them.

All this worldly wisdom was once the unamiable heresy of some wise man.

Truth, Goodness, Beauty—those celestial thrins,
Continually are born; e'en now the Universe,
With thousand throats, and eke with greener smiles,
Its joy confesses at their recent birth.
—Journal entry, June 14, 1838

Falsehoods that glare and dazzle are sloped toward us, reflecting full in our faces even the light of the sun. Wait till sunset, or go round them, and the falsity will be apparent.

—Journal entry, 1840

We Yankees are not so far from right, who answer one question by asking another. Yes and No are lies. A true answer will not aim to establish anything, but rather to set all well afloat. All answers are in the future, and day answereth to day. Do we think we can anticipate them?

—Journal entry, 1840

Poetry *implies* the whole truth. Philosophy *expresses* a particle of it.

—Journal entry, 1852

Every poet has trembled on the verge of science.

—Journal entry, 1852

I am sorry to think that you do not get a man's most effective criticism until you provoke him. Severe truth is expressed with some bitterness.

—Journal entry, 1854

Our life is frittered away by detail. An honest man has hardly need to count more than his ten fingers, or in extreme cases he may add his ten toes, and lump the rest. Simplicity, simplicity, simplicity! I say, let your affairs be as two or three, and not a hundred or a thousand; instead of a million count half a dozen, and keep your accounts on the thumb nail. In the midst of this chopping sea of civilized life, such are the clouds and storms and quicksands and thousand-and-one items to be allowed for, that a man has to live, if he would not founder and go to the bottom and not make his port at all, by dead reckoning, and he must be a great calculator indeed who succeeds. Simplify, simplify. Instead of three meals a day, if it be necessary eat but one; instead of a hundred dishes, five; and reduce other things in proportion.

—*Walden*, "Where I Lived, and What I Lived For," 1854

In the savage state, every family owns a shelter as good as the best, and sufficient for its coarser and simpler wants; though the birds of the air have their nests, and the foxes their holes, and the savages their wigwams, in modern civilized society not more than one half the families own a shelter. In the large towns and cities, where civilization especially prevails, the number of those who own a shelter is a very small fraction of a whole. The rest pay an annual tax for this outside garment of all, become indispensable summer and winter, which would buy a village of Indian wigwams, but now helps to keep them poor as long as they live. I do not mean to insist here on the disadvantage of hiring compared with owning, but it is evident that the savage owns his shelter because it costs little, while the civilized man hires his commonly because he cannot afford to own it; nor can he, in the long run, any better afford to hire. . . . An average house in this neighborhood costs perhaps eight hundred dollars, and to lay up this sum will take from ten to fifteen years of the laborer's life.

—*Walden*, "Economy," 1854

I used to see a large box by the railroad, six feet long by three feet wide, in which the laborers locked up their tools at night, and it suggested to me that every man who was pushed might get such a one for a dollar, and, having bored a few auger holes in it, to admit the air at least, get into it when it rained and at night, and hook down the lid, and so have freedom in his love, and in his soul be free. This did not appear the worst, nor by any means a despicable alternative. You could sit up as late as you pleased, and, whenever you got up, go abroad without any landlord or house-lord dogging you for rent. Many a man is harassed to death to pay the rent of a larger and more luxurious box who would not have frozen to death in such a box as this. I am far from jesting. Economy is a subject which admits of being treated with levity, but it cannot so be disposed of. A comfortable house for a rude and hardy race, that lived mostly out of doors, was once made here almost entirely out of such materials as Nature furnished ready to their lands. Gookin, who was superintendent of the Indians subject to Massachusetts Colony, writing in 1674, says, "The best of their houses are covered very neatly, tight and warm, with barks of trees, slipped from their bodies at those seasons when the sap is up,

and made into great flakes, with pressure of weighty timber, when they are green. . . . The meaner sort are covered with mats which they make of a kind of bulrush, and are also indifferently tight and warm, but not so good as the former. . . . Some I have seen, sixty or a hundred feet long and thirty feet broad. . . . I have often lodged in their wigwams, and found them as warm as the best English houses."

—*Walden*, "Economy," 1854

To be a philosopher is not merely to have subtle thoughts nor even to found a school but so to love wisdom as to live according to its dictates, a life of simplicity, independence, magnanimity, and trust. It is to solve some of the problems of life, not only theoretically but practically.

—*Walden*, "Economy," 1854

I had three pieces of limestone on my desk, but I was terrified to find that they required to be dusted daily, when the furniture of my mind was all undusted still, and I threw them out the window in disgust. How, then, could I have a furnished house? I would rather sit in the open air, for no dust gathers on the grass, unless where man has broken ground.

—*Walden*, "Economy," 1854

I know of one or two families, at least, in this town, who, for nearly a generation, have been wishing to sell their house on the outskirts and move into the village, but have not been able to accomplish it, and only death will set them free.

—*Walden*, "Economy," 1854

Thoreau and the Art of Life

I would observe, by the way, that it costs me nothing for curtains, for I have no gazers to shut out but the sun and moon, and I am willing that they should look in. The moon will not sour milk nor taint meat of mine, nor will the sun injure my furniture or fade my carpet, and if he is sometimes too warm a friend, I find it still better economy to retreat behind some curtain which nature has provided, than to add a single item to the details of housekeeping. A lady once offered me a mat, but as I had no room to spare within the house, nor time to spare within or without to shake it, I declined it, preferring to wipe my feet on the sod before my door. It is best to avoid the beginnings of evil.

　　　—*Walden*, "Economy," 1854

It is always a recommendation to me to know that a man has ever been poor, has been regularly born into this world, knows the language. I require to be assured of certain philosophers that they once have been barefooted, footsore, have eaten a crust because they had nothing better, and know what sweetness resides in it.

　　　—Journal entry, October 20, 1855

What is often called poverty, but which is a simpler and truer relation to nature, gives a peculiar relish to life, just as to be kept short gives us an appetite for food.

　　　—Journal entry, 1859

The deep places in the river are not so obvious as the shallow ones and can only be found by carefully probing it. So perhaps it is with human nature.

　　　—Journal entry, 1859

I think it will be found that he who speaks with [the] most authority on a given subject is not ignorant of what has been said by his predecessors. He will take his place in a regular order, and substantially add his own knowledge to the knowledge of previous generations.

　　　—Journal entry, 1859

Relations with Oneself

The path of joy is one of knowing who you are and living it.
It requires befriending yourself.

One's friendship with oneself, based largely on solitude, determines what we do with our life and is the basis of real success. Ultimately, we live in our own reality, and our inner life determines that reality.

Not until we are lost do we begin to understand ourselves.

Things do not change; we change.

Our truest life is when we are in dreams awake.

Do not lose hold of your dreams or aspirations. For if you do, you may still exist but you have ceased to live.

Thought is the sculptor who can create the person you want to be.

I do not know how to distinguish between our waking life and a dream. Are we not always living the life that we imagine we are?

What lies behind us and what lies ahead of us are tiny matters compared to what lives within us.

We are constantly invited to be who we are.

Dreams are the touchstones of our character.

Each man's necessary path, though as obscure and apparently uneventful as that of a beetle in the grass, is the way to the deepest joys he is susceptible of; though he converses only with moles and fungi and disgraces his relatives, it is no matter if he knows what is steel to his flint.

I want to go soon and live away by the pond, where I shall hear only the wind whispering among the reeds. It will be success if I shall have left myself behind. But my friends ask what I will do when I get there. Will it not be employment enough to watch the progress of the seasons?

—Journal entry, 1841

A new moon visible in the east—how unexpectedly it always appears! You easily lose it in the sky. The whip-poor-will sings—but not so commonly as in the spring. The bats are active. The poet is a man who lives at last by watching his moods. An old poet comes at last to watch his moods as narrowly as a cat does a mouse.

—Journal entry, August 1851

Why should pensiveness be akin to sadness? There is a certain fertile sadness which I would not avoid, but rather earnestly seek. It is positively joyful to me. It saves my life from being trivial.

It plainly makes men sad to think. Hence *pensiveness* is akin to sadness.

—Journal entry, 1851

There is no glory so bright but the veil of business can hide it effectually. With most men life is postponed to some trivial business, and so therefore is heaven. Men think foolishly they may abuse and misspend life as they please and when they get to heaven turn over a new leaf.

—Journal entry, 1851

If I have got false teeth, I trust that I have not got a false conscience. It is safer to employ the dentist than the priest to repair the deficiencies of nature.

—Journal entry, 1851

I cannot conceive how a man can accomplish anything worthy of him, unless his very breath is sweet to him. He must be particularly alive.

—Journal entry, 1852

Public opinion is a weak tyrant compared with our own private opinion. What a man thinks of himself, that is what determines, or rather indicates, his fate.

—*Walden*, "Economy," 1854

It is easier to sail many thousand miles through cold and storm and cannibals . . . with five hundred men and boys to assist one, than it is to explore the private sea, the Atlantic and Pacific Ocean of one's being alone.

—*Walden*, "Conclusion," 1854

The man who goes alone can start today; but he who travels with another must wait till that other is ready.

—Journal entry, 1854

To Hubbard Bath Swamp by Boat.

There sits one by the shore who wishes to go with me, but I cannot think of it. I must be fancy-free. There is no such mote in the sky as a man who is not perfectly transparent to you—who has any opacity. I would rather attend to him earnestly for half an hour, on shore or elsewhere, and then dismiss him. He thinks I could merely take him into my boat and then not mind him. He does not realize that I should by the same act take him into my mind, where there is no room for him, and my bark would surely founder in such a voyage as I was contemplating. I know very well that I should never reach that expansion of the river I have in my mind.

—Journal entry, August 31, 1856

Thoreau and the Art of Life

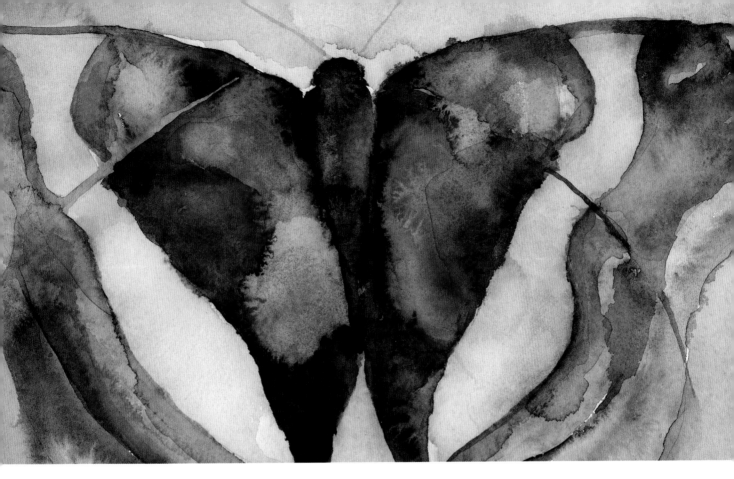

I ordinarily plod along a sort of whitewashed prison entry, subject to some indifferent or even groveling mood. I do not distinctly realize my destiny. I have turned down my light to the merest glimmer and am doing some task which I have set myself. I take incredibly narrow views, live on the limits, and have no recollection of absolute truth. Mushroom institutions hedge me in. But suddenly, in some fortunate moment, the voice of eternal wisdom reaches me even, in the strain of the sparrow, and liberates me, whets and clarifies my senses, makes me a competent witness.

—Journal entry, 1857

Do not despair of life. You have no doubt force enough to overcome your obstacles. Think of the fox prowling through wood and field in a winter night for something to satisfy his hunger. Notwithstanding cold and the hounds and traps, his race survives. I do not believe any of them ever committed suicide. I saw this afternoon where probably a fox had rolled some small carcass in the snow.

—Journal entry, 1857

Relations with Oneself

Inner Peace, Leisure, Serenity, Silence, Time

Make time for silence. Adopt a thoughtful rhythm to your work and life.

Thoreau believed that the true nature of silence and time were not knowable, but that a peaceful and serene life required making time for silence and a slower rhythm in one's life.

You cannot perceive beauty but with a serene mind.

Glances of true beauty can be seen in the faces of those who live in true meekness.

A broad margin of leisure is as beautiful in a man's life as in a book.

He enjoys true leisure who has time to improve his soul's estate.

Work, work, work. It would be glorious to see mankind at leisure for once.

Every rational man, let his business or station in life be what it may, should . . . at least once a year withdraw himself from the numerous connections and allurements that are apt to give us too great a fondness for life; he should take time to reflect, as a rational being ought to do, and consider well the end of his being.

As if you could kill time without injuring eternity.

Silence is the universal refuge, the sequel to all dull discourses and all foolish acts, a balm to our every chagrin, as welcome after satiety as after disappointment.

Silence is the communing of a conscious soul with itself. If the soul attends for a moment to its own infinity, then and there is silence. She is audible to all men, at all times, in all places, and if we will we may always hearken to her admonitions.

—Journal entry, 1838

It takes a man to make a room silent.

　　　—Journal entry, February 9, 1839

All things are in revolution; it is the one law of nature by which order is preserved, and time itself lapses and is measured. Yet some things men will do from age to age, and some things they will not do.

　　　—Journal entry, sometime in the 1840s

When I detect a beauty in any of the recesses of nature, I am reminded by the serene and retired spirit in which it requires to be contemplated, of the inexpressible privacy of life—how silent and unambitious it is. The beauty there is in mosses will have to be considered from the holiest, quietest nook.

The gods delight in stillness; they say, "'St, 'st." My truest, serenest moments are too still for emotion; they have woolen feet. In all our lives we live under the hill, and if we are not gone we live there still.

　　　—"Natural History of Massachusetts," 1842

Waves of a serene life pass over us from time to time, like flakes of sunlight over the fields in cloudy weather.

　　　—*A Week on the Concord and Merrimack Rivers*, 1849

To be calm, to be serene! There is the calmness of the lake when there is not a breath of wind; there is the calmness of a stagnant ditch. So is it with us. Sometimes we are clarified and calmed healthily, as we never were

Thoreau and the Art of Life

before in our lives, not by an opiate, but by some unconscious obedience to the all-just laws, so that we become like a still lake of purest crystal and without an effort our depths are revealed to ourselves. All the world goes by us and is reflected in our deeps. Such clarity! obtained by such pure means! by simple living, by honesty of purpose. We live and rejoice. I awoke into a music which no one by me heard. Whom shall I thank for it? The luxury of wisdom! the luxury of virtue! Are there any intemperate in these things? I feel my Maker blessing me. To the

sane man the world is a musical instrument. The very touch affords an exquisite pleasure.

—Journal entry, June 22, 1851

The longest silence is the most pertinent question most pertinently put. Emphatically silent. The most important question, whose answers concern us more than any, are never put in any other way.

—Journal entry, 1851

Inner Peace, Leisure, Serenity, Silence, Time

One of the most attractive things about the flowers is their beautiful reserve.

—Journal entry, 1853

I am sure that I never read any memorable news in a newspaper. If we read of one man robbed, one vessel wrecked, or one steamboat blown up, or one cow run over on the Western Railroad, or one mad dog killed, or one lot of grasshoppers in the winter—we never need read of another. One is enough. If you are acquainted with the principle, what do you care for a myriad instances and applications? To a philosopher all news, as it is called, is gossip, and they who edit it are old men over their tea.

—*Walden*, "Where I Lived, and What I Lived For," 1854

Time is cheap and rather insignificant. It matters not whether it is a river which changes from side to side in a geological period or an eel that wriggles past in an instant.

—Journal entry, 1855

I did not read books the first summer; I hoed beans. Nay, I often did better than this. There were times when I could not afford to sacrifice the bloom of the present moment to any work, whether of the brain or the hands. I love a broad margin to my life. Sometimes, in a summer morning, having taken my accustomed bath, I sat in my sunny doorway from sunrise till noon, rapt in a reverie, amidst the pines and hickories and sumacs, in undisturbed solitude and stillness, while the birds sang around or flitted noiseless through the house, until by the sun falling in at my west window, or the noise of some traveler's wagon on the distant highway, I was reminded of the lapse of time. I grew in those seasons like corn in the night, and they were far better than any work of the hands would have been. They were not time subtracted from my life, but so much over and above my usual allowance. I realized what the Orientals mean by contemplation and the forsaking of works. For the most part, I minded not how the hours went. The day advanced as if to light some work of mine; it was morning, and lo, now it is evening, and nothing memorable is accomplished. Instead of singing like the birds, I silently smiled at my incessantly good fortune. As the sparrow had its trill, sitting on the hickory before my door, so had I my chuckle or sup-pressed warble which he might hear out of my nest. My days were not days of the week, bearing the stamp of any heathen deity, nor were they minced into hours and fretted by the ticking of a clock; for I lived like the Puri Indians, of whom it is said that "for yester-day, today, and tomorrow they have only one word, and they express the variety of meaning by pointing backward for yesterday, forward for tomorrow, and overhead for the passing day." This was sheer idleness to my fellow townsmen, no doubt; but if the birds and flowers had tried me by their standard, I should not have been found wanting. A man must find his occasions in himself, it is true. The natural day is very calm, and will hardly improve his indolence.

—*Walden*, "Sounds," 1854

In any weather, at any hour of the day or night, I have been anxious to improve the nick of time, and notch it on my stick too; to stand on the meeting of two eternities, the past and future, which is precisely the present moment; to toe that line. You will pardon some obscurities, for there are more secrets in my trade than in most men's, and yet not voluntarily kept, but insepa-rable from its very nature.

—*Walden*, "Economy," 1854

Consider the turtle. A whole summer—June, July, and August—is not too good nor too much to hatch a turtle in. Perchance you have worried yourself, despaired of the world, meditated the end of life, and all things seemed rushing to destruction; but nature has steadily and serenely advanced with a turtle's pace.

    —Journal entry, 1856

My mother was telling tonight of the sounds she used to hear summer nights when she was young and lived on the Virginia Road—the lowing of cows, or cackling of geese, or the beating of a drum as far off as Hildreth's, but above all Joe Merriam whistling to his team, for he was an admirable whistler. Says she used to get up at midnight and go and sit on the doorstep when all in the house were asleep, and she could hear nothing in the world but the ticking of the clock in the house behind her.

    —Journal entry, May 26, 1857

A man must attend to Nature closely for many years to know when, as well as where, to look for his objects, since he must always anticipate her a little. Young men have not learned the phases of Nature; they do not know what constitutes a year, or that one year is like another. I would know when in the year to expect certain thoughts and moods, as the sportsman knows when to look for plover.

    —Journal entry, 1859

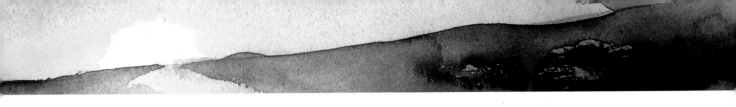

Bibliography

Abbey, Edward. *The Best of Edward Abbey.* 2nd ed. San Francisco: Sierra Club Books, 2005.

Emerson, Edward Waldo. *Henry Thoreau as Remembered by a Young Friend.* Concord, MA: Thoreau Foundation, 1968.

Harding, Walter, ed. *Thoreau as Seen by His Contemporaries.* Rev. ed. of *Thoreau, Man of Concord,* 1960. New York: Dover Publications, 1989.

Hawthorne, Nathaniel. *The American Notebooks.* New Haven, CT: Yale University Press, 1932.

Krutch, Joseph Wood, ed. *Thoreau: Walden and Other Writings.* New York: Bantam Books, 1965.

McLaughlin, Walt. *A Natural Wisdom: Gleanings from the Journals of Henry David Thoreau.* North Ferrisburg, VT: Heron Dance Press, 2004.

Olson, Sigurd F. *Reflections from the North Country.* New York: Knopf, 1976.

Teale, Edwin Way. *The Lost Woods: Adventures of a Naturalist.* New York: Dodd, Mead & Company, 1945.

Thoreau, Henry David. *Civil Disobedience, and Other Essays.* "Civil Disobedience" (1849), "Slavery in Massachusetts" (1854), "Walking" (1863), "Life without Principle" (1863). New York: Dover Publications, 1993.

——. "The Commercial Spirit of Modern Times, Considered in Its Influence on the Moral Character of a Nation." Commencement speech, Harvard University, Cambridge, MA, 1837.

——. *Familiar Letters.* Edited by F.B. Sanborn. New York: AMS Press, 1982.

——. *The Heart of Thoreau's Journals.* 2nd ed. Edited by Odell Shepard. New York: Dover Publications, 1961.

——. *The Maine Woods: By Henry D. Thoreau, Author of "A Week on the Concord and Merrimack Rivers," "Walden," "Excursions," etc., etc* [sic]. Edited by S. Thoreau and W.E. Channing. Boston: Ticknor and Fields, 1864.

——. *The Natural History Essays.* "Natural History of Massachusetts" (1842), "Walking" (1863). Salt Lake City: Peregrine Smith, 1980.

——. *Walden.* Boston: Ticknor and Fields, 1862.

——. *Walden.* New York: C. E. Merrill Co., 1910.

——. *A Week on the Concord and Merrimack Rivers.* New York: George P. Putnam, 1849.

List of Illustrations

All the watercolors in this book are by Roderick MacIver, founder of Heron Dance. Select watercolors from this list are available as full-color, limited-edition prints on the Heron Dance Web site (www.herondance.org) by typing the title in the search bar. If you have trouble finding the image you would like or do not have access to the Internet, please call Heron Dance toll-free at 888-304-3766 or send an e-mail to heron@herondance.org. Thank you.

Heron Dance

HERON DANCE Press & Art Studio is a nonprofit 501(c)(3) organization founded in 1995.

HERON DANCE explores the beauty and mystery of the natural world through art and words. It is a work of love, an effort to produce something that is thought-provoking and beautiful. We offer *A Pause for Beauty, The HERON DANCE Nature Art Journal,* and note cards, books, and calendars.

We invite you to visit us at www.herondance.org to view the hundreds of watercolors by Roderick MacIver and to browse the hundreds of pages of book excerpts, poetry, essays, and interviews of authors and artists.

Nonprofit Donations

HERON DANCE donates thousands of note cards and the use of hundreds of images to small nonprofits every year. We also donate books and prints for fund-raisers. Please contact us for more information.

The HERON DANCE Nature Art Journal

Available by subscription, *The HERON DANCE Nature Art Journal* is a 72-page full-color journal published twice a year that features nature watercolors by Roderick MacIver throughout. In its latest incarnation, it is a semi-fictional account of a wild artist who loves wild places, wild rivers, and wild women. It is a celebration of the gift of life! Visit our Web site to get more information (click Subscribe or Renew, then Plans for the HERON DANCE Nature Art Journal) or to sign up.

Our Free Weekly E-newsletter: *A Pause for Beauty*

Each issue features a new watercolor or acrylic ink painting, and a poem, quotation, or reflection. Over 25,000 people have signed up for *A Pause for Beauty.* To sign up or view our archives, please visit our Web site.

Watercolors by Roderick MacIver

Hundreds of nature watercolors are available as signed limited-edition prints and originals at www.herondance.org.

Online Gallery

We offer note cards, daybooks, calendars, address books, and blank journals that feature Roderick MacIver watercolors, along with inspirational titles from HERON DANCE Press, including *The Heron Dance Book of Love and Gratitude.*

HERON DANCE Community

The HERON DANCE community consists of over 12,000 subscribers to our print journal and over 25,000 readers of our free weekly e-mail *A Pause for Beauty.* To connect with other Heron Dancers, please visit our Facebook page. Links to that page and to founder Rod MacIver's page can be found by going to the HERON DANCE Web site, then clicking About HERON DANCE and then Connect with Other Heron Dancers.

- www.herondance.org
- 888-304-3766
- heron@herondance.org

Artist and Editor
Roderick MacIver

RODERICK MACIVER has been a self-employed artist and writer since 1995, when he founded the Heron Dance newsletter to celebrate the seeker's journey and the spirit and beauty of all that is wild. He began publishing books under Heron Dance Press in 2002. MacIver's words and watercolors are inspired by a love of wild places and the peace and rhythm he finds there. His watercolors are the perfect medium to express his reverence for nature, reflecting a simple flow and simplicity. He has donated thousands of his images to grassroots wilderness protection groups and these organizations, along with other nonprofits, have used his art in their newsletters, on their Web sites, and in their outreach efforts. Born in Canada, MacIver currently splits his time between Heron Dance Press in Vermont and his studio in New York's Adirondacks.

Artist's Perspective

Erase the lines: I pray you not to love classifications.
The thing is like a river, from source to sea-mouth
One flowing life.

—Robinson Jeffers, Monument

Since about the age of eight, my life and art have been nourished and inspired by time in wild places, by cycles larger than the concerns of man. The deep silence and deep peace of wild places, and yes even the great struggle to cling to life, the precious gift of life, are at the center of my work. I try to express reverence for the mystery and beauty of wild places. I try, through my painting and writing, to honor the places I love and the sense of freedom I've found there.

Of the Robinson Jeffers quote, perhaps the words that most puzzle and inspire me are "one flowing life." I know what he means but cannot explain it. It is part of the mystery. In my art, I try to flow, to capture the essence and spirit of that great flowing life, of struggle and silence and peace.

I try to express the spirit and essence rather than the detail. I try and try and fail and try again with the hope that over time the spirit of what Robinson Jeffers refers to as "the river . . . one flowing life" might gradually emerge.

—Roderick MacIver, Monkton, Vermont

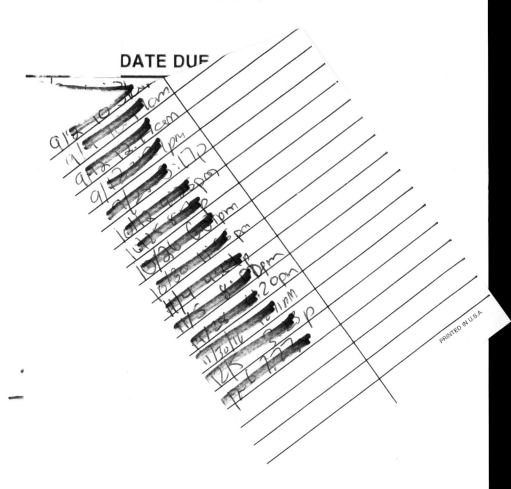

DATE DUE

PRINTED IN U.S.A.